*Millennium*

# PHILADELPHIA

*Updated & Expanded*

# *Millennium* PHILADELPHIA

## *Updated & Expanded*

By the staff of
**The Philadelphia Inquirer**

Camino Books, Inc.
Philadelphia

# *Millennium* PHILADELPHIA

*Staff for this book:*

*Editor*
**Avery Rome**

*Art Director / Designer*
**Kevin Burkett**

*Photo Editor*
**Clem Murray**

*Copy Editor*
**Addam Schwartz**

*Additional Staff (for original printing)*
**Lois Wark**
**David Milne**
**Ed Hille**
**Tom Steacy**
**Ed Voves**
**Denise Boal**

**Cover photos** (*not elsewhere in book*)**:**
(Top) A view of Philadelphia, circa 1905, looking north from Broad and Locust toward City Hall.
HISTORICAL SOCIETY OF PENNSYLVANIA / PENROSE COLLECTION

(Front inside flap) The William Penn statue sits in the City Hall courtyard before being hoisted atop the tower.
INQUIRER ARCHIVES

(Back inside flap) The William Penn statue, in 2002, with the crescent moon rising in the background.
THE PHILADELPHIA INQUIRER / DAVID SWANSON

**Page 2 photo:**
The statue of William Penn atop City Hall is overshadowed by One Liberty Place; 1991 photo.
THE PHILADELPHIA INQUIRER / MICHAEL MALLY

**Facing page:**
The William Penn statue as seen looking up from the City Hall observation deck.
THE PHILADELPHIA INQUIRER / RICHARD M. TITLEY

Visit The Inquirer online at **www.philly.com**

1 2 3 4 5  11 10 09 08

*Library of Congress Cataloging-in-Publication Data*
Millennium Philadelphia / by the staff of the Philadelphia Inquirer. — Updated and expanded.
  p. cm.
  Includes index.
  ISBN 978-1-933822-11-2 (alk. paper)
  1. Philadelphia (Pa.)—History—20th century—Pictorial works.
  2. Philadelphia (Pa.)—History—21st century—Pictorial works.
  3. Philadelphia (Pa.)—Pictorial works.
  I. Philadelphia Inquirer (Firm)
  II. Title.
  F158.37.M55 2008
  974.8'11043—dc22          2007024070

*For information write*
Publisher
Camino Books, Inc.
P.O. Box 59026
Philadelphia, Pa. 19102

www.caminobooks.com

Printed in China

# Contents

# Foreword

The staff of The Philadelphia Inquirer has revised the highly popular *Millennium Philadelphia: The Last One Hundred Years* with an added all-new full-color chapter covering the most significant events from 1999 to 2007. We have prepared this revised pictorial history in a deluxe paperbound edition, now expanded yet retaining all of the original photography and commentary that made it an important keepsake in households.

This unique volume captures all of the events that made big news in the city, suburbs and region. The Philadelphia Inquirer was there every step along the way. For anyone who currently lives here — or formerly lived here — this book captures the news and newsmakers of the region as no other book can do.

Back in 2006, I had the pleasure of bringing together a group of local investors — who, like this book, are totally committed to the region — to acquire The Philadelphia Inquirer. It is our hope to continue The Inquirer's great legacy and to make some history of our own. We believe in this city and the important role the press plays in bringing people together.

Our hope is that by looking back at what has made this city great, we might find the pride and inspiration to continue that mission for many years to come and even to the end of this millennium.

Brian Tierney, Publisher

# The Changing City

O N DEC. 31, 1900, Philadelphia turned out en masse to meet the 20th century.

In other years, the celebration had centered around the Pennsylvania State House — what we now call Independence Hall. But that was an old-hat building, in an old-hat section of town. For this special New Year's Eve, the party shifted to the heart of the new Philadelphia. To City Hall.

Nearly complete after 30 years in the making, this gargantuan granite-and-marble crag of a building boasted the tallest masonry tower in the world. On New Year's Eve, it was bedecked with strings of lights, cascading from the rim of Billy Penn's hat to the street. And it was wired with explosives.

City fathers had allocated $1,500 for fireworks. Their plan for the first 10 minutes of the new century was to turn night into day. Newspapers predicted the "fountain of fire" would be visible for 20 miles on every side — startling cows from Collingswood to Wawa.

Nature had other plans: fog. Dense, moist, and gray, it enshrouded the city, swallowing up the bursts of light. Not that the thousands in the street minded. They oohed and aahed at the lights and fireworks, clapped time to the music, lined up to

**The place to meet** was at the eagle at Wanamakers.

**In 1907, the automobile** was a rarity. Most of Philadelphia's 1.3 million residents lived in Center City and nearby industrial areas. This is Market Street, looking east toward the Delaware River.

shake hands with Mayor Samuel H. Ashbridge, stationed before a blazing fire to receive the throng.

Poised on the lip of a new century, Philadelphia felt a need to boast. And why not?

The population had nearly doubled in 30 years, to 1.3 million souls in 1900. The city was optimistic, brash and sooty. It moved to the clang of the forge, the hum of machinery. Industry was the city's backbone, its pride, its future.

Dimly, but surely, people could see great things coming. In the *North American*, the scrappiest of the city's half-dozen daily newspapers, cartoonist George McDougall peered into the future and offered his vision of Philadelphia in 2001. It was a marvelous place — with huge winged flying ships, a subterranean railroad to China, moving sidewalks, and — can you believe this — a baby carriage being pushed by a man!

We can laugh at our predecessors' mix of naivete, prescience and optimism. But, in fairness, how could anyone then imagine what the future would bring to Philadelphia?

The arrival of skyscrapers that eventually would dwarf City Hall. The dominance of the automobile, and its power

**The first Mummers Parade** was in 1901 and included this group of men in blackface and dresses.

THE LIBRARY COMPANY OF PHILADELPHIA / PHOTO-ILLUSTRATORS

to change lives and landscapes. The decline of the city, the rise of the suburbs.

From that foggy New Year's Eve to today, Philadelphia has gone from industrial to post-industrial, from "corrupt and contented" Republican to overwhelmingly Democratic, from the "Quaker City" ruled by a WASP elite to one that has had as its last five mayors Americans of Irish, Italian, African and Jewish descent.

On New Year's Day 1901, the Radnor Hunt Club held its traditional fox hunt, beginning near Bryn Mawr and ranging as far as West Chester. There was plenty of open land for the horses to traverse. Ninety percent of the region's people lived within less than a mile of City Hall. Today, 90 percent live outside that circle. Philadelphia, writ large, is begin-

ning to encroach on Lancaster County. (By the way, in 1901 the fox escaped. Today, he'd never make it across Route 30 alive.)

For the first three decades, until the Depression shut things down, the city stretched its muscles: building roads and bridges, subways and elevated railroads to the far reaches of the city, and beyond.

While the automobile was accelerating change, railroads were doing the same. The Pennsylvania Railroad had created the Main Line, and here's how you remembered the stations: "Old Maids Never Wed and Have Babies, Period" (Overbrook, Merion, Narberth, Wynnewood, Ardmore, Haverford, Bryn Mawr, Paoli).

The generations turned over, new people arrived, living out their lives in many of the same homes, the same public places where we live today. In life, change is the only constant — though we can delude ourselves into believing in permanence. The city helps fool us on that account, layering the past with the present. The house where I live was built in 1844 as a shared hovel bought by a half-dozen workingmen, their wives and sweethearts likely across the ocean in Ireland, waiting for them to send money for passage.

Our ties to Philadelphia's past may be as thick as a dozen generations, or as tenuous as arrival on yesterday's jet. But the lines flow back, even if we cannot see them. As this book will prove, the story is not only about famous people and great events. The block lady briskly sweeping her sidewalk is part of it. The horse-drawn fire truck roaring down the street is part of it. Sports heroes and singers, cops and children, big-time pols and small-time mobsters are part of it. Even a royal princess, improbably named Kelly, is part of it.

So, sit with us awhile as we conjure up the past century, to present the people and the stories that make this city unique. We'll journey backward together. Through a Philadelphia century. ∎

**Philadelphia greeted the 20th century** on Jan. 1, 1901, with an elaborate display of fireworks and with electric lights draped on City Hall.

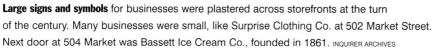

**Large signs and symbols** for businesses were plastered across storefronts at the turn of the century. Many businesses were small, like Surprise Clothing Co. at 502 Market Street. Next door at 504 Market was Bassett Ice Cream Co., founded in 1861. INQUIRER ARCHIVES

**Philadelphia remains a walking city.**
Here, pedestrians and horse-drawn cabs make their way past Independence Hall, circa 1900. The view looks east on Chestnut Street.

TEMPLE URBAN ARCHIVES / THE EVENING BULLETIN

**The first automobiles appeared** on city streets in 1899. By 1919, there were 100,000 cars and 7,000 trucks, including these Wanamakers delivery vehicles.

THE PHILADELPHIA INQUIRER

**In 1915 the Masonic Temple,** just north of City Hall, towers over the statue of Gen. George B. McClellan, Philadelphia-born Civil War commander.

HISTORICAL SOCIETY OF PENNSYLVANIA / BOIES PENROSE COLLECTION, PHILIP WALLACE

**When it opened in 1926, the Delaware River Bridge** was the world's longest suspension bridge, at nearly two miles. Construction began in 1919 and cost $37 million. The bridge was renamed for Benjamin Franklin in 1955. Here, political leaders from Philadelphia and Camden, N.J., check construction via a footbridge.

**On opening day,** July 1, 1926, an estimated 250,000 people paraded across the Delaware River Bridge, "a mighty throng 35 abreast," reported *The Philadelphia Inquirer*. The chief engineer, a Polish immigrant named Ralph Modjeski, proclaimed that his bridge could hold the entire population of Camden "without showing any strain." He was better than his word. Camden's 1920 population was 116,309.

**The bridge toll was 25 cents** — and that was controversial. The bridge was a joint effort; New Jersey pressed for tolls, Pennsylvania and Philadelphia wanted the bridge "to remain forever free." In order to get it built, Pennsylvania relented.

**Rowing on the Delaware** was a common pleasure. This is in the Port Richmond/ Kensington area, circa 1910, with the Cramp shipyard in the background.

**For generations, the Delaware River**
provided Philadelphians with a great place
for swimming and boating. But in 1895,
the state fish commission noted the discharge
of coal oil and other "dangerous poisons"
into the river. By the 1940s, 500 million gallons
a year of raw sewage and industrial waste
were being dumped into the Delaware.
Carefree "skinny-dipping," like this 1918 scene
at Pier 126 North near Allegheny Avenue,
became a joy of the past.

**As seen looking east from Logan Circle in 1929,** Philadelphia's skyline was beginning to change. The recently built (1925) office of the Insurance Company of North America (at right), 16th and Arch Streets, joined the Cathedral Basilica of Saints Peter and Paul and City Hall. INQUIRER ARCHIVES

**The Benjamin Franklin Parkway,** conceived as Philadelphia's Champs Elysée, was completed in 1917. During the 1920s, imposing cultural buildings began to rise along its course: the Free Library of Philadelphia, 1927 (at right); the Franklin Institute, 1934 (center left); and, at the end of the vista, the Museum of Art, 1928.

THE PHILADELPHIA INQUIRER

**A view of the Schuylkill and Boathouse Row** from the Waterworks in 1938. There are now 10 boathouses, nine of them owned by rowing clubs, one publicly owned. The famous trim of light bulbs was added in 1979 and replaced by LEDs 18 years later. THE PHILADELPHIA INQUIRER

**For rowhouse families,** maintaining the home and neighborhood became a point of pride, as these residents of the 1000 block of Fitzwater Street in South Philadelphia demonstrate in May 1949. Because there were so many rowhouses, rather than high-rise tenements, Philadelphia had a higher rate of home-ownership than any other big city. THE PHILADELPHIA INQUIRER

**In the early 1900s,** waves of Russian Jews and immigrants from Southern Italy crowded into South Philadelphia. Many of the Jewish families moved on to Northern Liberties and Logan. The Tutendari family, shown about 1920 at 1009 Montrose Street, settled in what came to be known as Little Italy.

TEMPLE URBAN ARCHIVES / PUBLIC HOUSING AUTHORITY

**Concern for the have-nots** led the Octavia Hill Association to promote better housing conditions for the poor. This photo was taken around 1900 to document an area described as "Negro Quarters," believed to be either Lombard or South Streets. For three rooms, families paid rent of $2 a week.

TEMPLE URBAN ARCHIVES / PUBLIC HOUSING AUTHORITY

**In 1907, when members of the Benevolent Protective Order of the Elks** held their national convention in Philadelphia, Strawbridge & Clothier decked itself out in their honor, including stuffed elks. So did Lit Brothers and Gimbels, across Market Street. TEMPLE URBAN ARCHIVES

**Movie palaces made downtown an entertainment mecca.** Opulent theaters like the Mastbaum and the Erlanger presented live entertainment, as well as films. Here, patrons line up at the Stanley, 19th and Market, to buy tickets for Cecil B. DeMille's 1921 silent drama *Forbidden Fruit.* HISTORICAL SOCIETY OF PENNSYLVANIA / SARGENT BELL COLLECTION

**The Pennsylvania Railroad's Broad Street Station,** opened in 1881, dominated Market Street west of City Hall until 1952, when it was demolished. Elevated track behind the station, which blocked north-south traffic, was known as the "Chinese wall." Penn Center is now on the site. INQUIRER ARCHIVES

**Philadelphia has long had a sizable African-American population.** Employment in professional positions was difficult to come by. In 1881, the city hired its first black patrolmen — four. When this photo was taken around 1905, their numbers were still small. INQUIRER ARCHIVES

**During the 1920s and '30s,** efforts were made to enhance police performance. Better pay, training, and equipment — like the submachine gun being displayed by this motorcycle squad in 1929 — raised effectiveness. But a corruption scandal in 1928 and difficulty enforcing Prohibition laws dented the department's image.

THE PHILADELPHIA INQUIRER

**Horse-drawn fire teams** began to be replaced with motor trucks in 1908. But some horses continued to take firefighters into action until 1928, when the last of them were retired to Chesterbrook Farms near Berwyn, Pa.

TEMPLE URBAN ARCHIVES / THE EVENING BULLETIN

**Dock Street,** which stretched three blocks from Sansom to Spruce between Water and Third, was the produce center until the new Food Distribution Center in South Philadelphia opened in 1959. The old market (shown in 1925) had been torn down by 1962, when Society Hill Towers rose on the site. INQUIRER ARCHIVES

**Philadelphia International Airport** began as Southwest Airport. It was renamed for Mayor S. Davis Wilson in the 1930s, and got its present name in 1953. Here, aircraft of the Pennsylvania National Guard give a demonstration in 1938. THE PHILADELPHIA INQUIRER

**Cargo ships line up in the Delaware** in 1955, with the city skyline in the background. Facing stiff competition from other East Coast ports, Philadelphia launched a major dredging project between 1898 and 1912 to make the Delaware navigable for modern tankers and freighters.

**The PSFS Building** at 1212 Market Street, a modernist masterpiece, was the first U.S. skyscraper built in the International Style. The 36-story building was designed by George Howe and William Lescaze and completed in the Depression year of 1932 — when banks were in low repute. Atop the Philadelphia Saving Fund Society Building, the PSFS letters are 27 feet high. In 2000, the office tower reopened as the Loews Philadelphia Hotel.

CORBIS-BETTMANN ARCHIVES

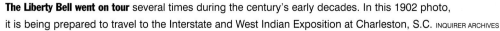

**The Liberty Bell went on tour** several times during the century's early decades. In this 1902 photo, it is being prepared to travel to the Interstate and West Indian Exposition at Charleston, S.C. INQUIRER ARCHIVES

**In 1952 the state of Pennsylvania demolished** three blocks of old Victorian structures to create Independence Mall. Four years earlier, the federal government had assumed control of Independence Hall, Carpenters' Hall, the First Bank of the United States, and other historic buildings.

**The restaurant that Joseph V. Horn and Frank Hardart Jr. opened** at 818 Chestnut Street in 1902 transformed their industry. It was the Automat, the nation's first fast-food outlet. It closed in 1968.

THE LIBRARY COMPANY OF PHILADELPHIA / PHOTO ILLUSTRATORS

**Soft pretzels, water ice, hot chestnuts and ethnic food** are specialties of the city's street vendors. TEMPLE URBAN ARCHIVES / THE EVENING BULLETIN

**The Italian Market,** at Ninth and Christian Streets, preserves much of the rough-and-ready atmosphere of street life in early 20th-century Philadelphia. It is shown here in 1973. THE PHILADELPHIA INQUIRER / CHARLES W. JAMES

**Since 1893, the Reading Terminal Market** has provided fresh produce to busy commuters. A major renovation in the 1990s and proximity to the new Convention Center have given the old market new life. In 1948, workers prepare turkeys for shoppers. THE PHILADELPHIA INQUIRER / HOWARD HAMBURGER

**With the end of World War II, nylon stockings** again became available — and there were long lines. In March 1946 customers wait to buy them — one pair each — at a shop on Pacific Street in North Philadelphia. Note: Only 6,000 pairs available. THE PHILADELPHIA INQUIRER / HOWARD HAMBURGER

**Chestnut Hill, with its stately homes** of Wissahickon schist and elegant shops along Germantown Avenue, has preserved its colonial ambience. A savvy merchants' association and a major project in the 1970s to replace crumbling cobblestones were key elements in this success. THE PHILADELPHIA INQUIRER / SARA KRULWICH

**The farmland beyond Frankford and Tacony in the Northeast** rapidly filled with new communities after the Second World War. Many of them had rural-sounding names, like Fox Chase and Somerton. Here, in 1951 residents of Oxford Circle tend their lawns, a major concern on the "crabgrass frontier."

TEMPLE URBAN ARCHIVES / THE EVENING BULLETIN

**In 1938, during the depths of the Depression,** there were still plenty of well-dressed shoppers, commuters and office workers crowding Market Street.

THE PHILADELPHIA INQUIRER

**Casino gambling arrived in Atlantic City** on May 26, 1978, when Resorts International opened. Twenty years later, 49,000 people were employed in the gambling industry, and property values had risen. But pockets of poverty remained.

THE PHILADELPHIA INQUIRER / AKIRA SUWA

**Lucy the Elephant has graced Margate since 1882.** James V. Lafferty used 1 million pieces of timber, 200 kegs of nails and 12,000 square feet of tin sheeting to build the 85-foot-high preposterous pachyderm.

THE PHILADELPHIA INQUIRER / WILLIAM AUGUSTINE

**Visitors to Atlantic City's Steel Pier** were treated to the improbable sight of young women riders diving their horses from a 40-foot platform into a tank of water. The act went on from 1929 until the Steel Pier closed in 1978. It reopened as an amusement pier in 1993. THE PHILADELPHIA INQUIRER

**It's "Philadelphia Day" down the shore!** These vacationers in Ocean City, N.J., are saluting the flag, and the city, on Aug. 20, 1936. It was a weekday, when most men were at work. THE PHILADELPHIA INQUIRER

**Suburban housing developments encroach on farmland** near Route 70 in Burlington County, N.J., in 1976. Between 1950 and 1970, Philadelphia's population declined 6 percent, while that of its suburban counties grew 30 percent. THE PHILADELPHIA INQUIRER / ROBERT L. MOONEY

**In the early 1960s, Society Hill Towers** — three 31-story buildings — rose above the townhouses of the historic district. Designed by I.M. Pei, the buildings were controversial because of the conflict in scale with their surroundings.

THE PHILADELPHIA INQUIRER / ROBERT L. MOONEY

**In December 1951, an open house at three sample Levittown homes** in Bucks County drew a crowd of 35,000. The first residents moved in the following June. Eventually 17,000 homes were built on the 5,750-acre site.

THE PHILADELPHIA INQUIRER

**The first section of the Schuylkill Expressway,** from King of Prussia to City Avenue, opened on Sept. 1, 1954. Drivers are exiting at City Avenue on opening day. Planners in 1950 estimated that 41,100 cars a day would use one stretch of the highway. A 1981 study counted 132,200 there.

THE PHILADELPHIA INQUIRER

**Construction of the Blue Route —**
Interstate 476 — was delayed for
more than 30 years by legal challenges
from towns and residents along its route.
First proposed in 1956, at a projected
cost of $40 million, the 21.5-mile high-
way linking the Pennsylvania Turnpike
and Interstate 95 finally opened in 1991.
By then, it cost $600 million —
or $5,503 a foot.

THE PHILADELPHIA INQUIRER / JONATHAN WILSON

**Interstate 95 through Philadelphia**
was completed in 1985, one of the last links
in the highway between Maine and Florida.
It took 25 years to build the 52 miles
that run through Philadelphia, Delaware,
and Bucks Counties. Construction cut
through crowded neighborhoods and
skirted the airport. In this 1968 photo,
land is being cleared for I-95, while,
one block east, landfill operations
are under way to create Penn's Landing.

THE PHILADELPHIA INQUIRER / JAMES L. McGARRITY

**The twin towers of Liberty Place** soar in this 1990 aerial view. Developer Willard Rouse 3rd and his architect, Helmut Jahn, in 1987 crashed through the height limit that Philadelphia had lived with for so long — the tradition that no building could be taller than the top of the William Penn statue on City Hall. One Liberty Place (left), at 17th and Market Streets, was topped off in May 1987 at 945 feet — 397 feet higher than City Hall. Two Liberty Place, 845 feet, was completed in 1990.

THE PHILADELPHIA INQUIRER / MICHAEL MALLY

**Alan Schaaf examines the bronze statue of William Penn** atop City Hall in July 1986 during the long restoration of the tower and sculpture designed by Alexander Milne Calder. Scaffolding remained around the 26-ton statue for more than a year, until a fund-raising drive featuring "Free Billy Penn" buttons helped liberate Philadelphia's founder in September 1987. THE PHILADELPHIA INQUIRER / KEN LAMBERT

**After a century, Philadelphia's skyline** is very different from that of 1901, when fireworks filled the sky over the city's tallest building, City Hall. It is barely identifiable in this 1995 aerial view of the city, shot from South Philadelphia.

THE PHILADELPHIA INQUIRER / ERIC MENCHER

# The Era of Muscle

AMERICA WAS PROSPEROUS and confident at the turn of the century. And so was Philadelphia.

Its population, which had soared over a million in 1890, would rise steadily until it exceeded two million in 1950. Its government was no great shakes; in fact, Lincoln Steffens, the muckraker, dismissed Philadelphia in 1903 as the "worst governed city in the country." But he also observed that it had "long enjoyed great and widely distributed prosperity," and its citizens gave him "a sense of more leisure and repose than any community I have ever dwelt in."

**Rail power** drove Philadelphia's economy. THE LIBRARY COMPANY OF PHILADELPHIA

Philadelphia's well-being sprang from its remarkable private sector.

Following the Civil War, entrepreneurs transformed the historic city into an industrial colossus, one that led all others in the making of ships and hats, locomotives and textiles. Its nickname, "Workshop of the World," was no idle boast, for Philadelphia's economy was the most diversified of any American metropolis.

Its workers forged steel, built trucks, knitted dresses, ran oil refineries. They made Baldwin locomotives, Stetson hats, Schmidt's beer, Bayuk

**As production begins to gear up** in anticipation of war, workers pour into the Budd Manufacturing Co. plant on Hunting Park Avenue in 1939. Budd, which made auto bodies and rail cars, converted to aircraft parts, tanks and munitions for World War II. INQUIRER ARCHIVES

cigars, Bassett's and Breyer's ice cream, Fels Naptha soap, Quaker lace, Atwater Kent radios, and countless other products for the booming nation. At the century's start, Philadelphia ranked third in the nation in number of workers and value of manufactured products.

It was a city of neighborhoods, the workers' small rowhouses clustered near the mills and factories. The Delaware River waterfront was becoming the American Clyde, the largest freshwater port on the East Coast, with 300 wharves and 159 piers.

Kensington, now an industrial wasteland of shattered factories, was home to the world's largest lace factory, the world's largest hat manufacturer, and scores of carpet makers.

At Broad and Spring Garden, thousands of Baldwin workers made Philadelphia first in the manufacture of steam locomotives. Railroading reached its zenith in this period, and the city was home to the nation's largest railroad company, the mighty Pennsylvania. Chartered in 1846, the Pennsy was locked in combat with the New York Central when its daring president, Alexander J. Cassatt, brother of impressionist artist Mary Cassatt, devised a bold plan to invade his rival's home turf. At Cassatt's direction, tunnels were dug under the Hudson and East Rivers, and the great Pennsylvania Station opened in Manhattan in 1910.

As the Pennsy expanded, so did other enterprises. Edward G. Budd, who came to Philadelphia as a 19-year-old apprentice machinist in 1899, started his own company in 1912. Soon he found customers among the nascent automakers in Detroit, and his business grew along with theirs. The Budd Co. gave America its first all-steel auto bodies; at its peak, Budd employed close to 20,000 workers.

J. Howard Pew in 1901 joined the Sun Oil Co., founded 15 years earlier by his father, Joseph N.

**Pennies by the bucket** roll from the U.S. Mint. It was on Spring Garden Street until 1969, when the Mint moved its operations to Fifth and Arch Streets.
INQUIRER ARCHIVES

Pew. It was the start of a 70-year association. His family's legacy is the Pew Charitable Trusts, one of the nation's largest charitable foundations.

By the time J. Howard Pew joined Sun Oil, John Batterson Stetson had already won fame as the world's premier hatmaker. He founded his business at Fifth Street and Montgomery Avenue in 1865.

Like most of the city's business leaders, Stetson was Protestant in his religion, conservative in his politics, and paternalistic in his business. He ran a Sunday school for 3,000 children and an afternoon kindergarten. He opened a hospital that treated 20,000 patients a year, subsidized his workers' lunches, and, in some cases, provided free life insurance.

But workers found their lives tightly constricted. Stetson's autocratic management style would lead to litigation today. It was spelled out in the agreement apprentices were obliged to sign when they were hired. On Dec. 19, 1904, 17-year-old Henry J. Levins signed one such agreement. In exchange for learning the "art, trade and mystery of felt hat finishing," Levins promised he would "serve his Masters faithfully, keep their secrets and obey their lawful commands." He could not "contract matrimony" during his four-year apprenticeship, or "play at cards, dice or any other unlawful game." He pledged not to "haunt ale houses, taverns or playhouses." His pay was $2 a week.

John B. Stetson died in 1906, but his company

**One of the region's biggest employers** was United States Steel's massive Fairless Works in Bucks County, which opened Dec. 11, 1952. During the 1950s and '60s, 10,000 steelworkers were employed. By the 1980s, foreign competition and new technology caused cuts; the steelmaking operation and pipe mill were closed in 1991. USX continues to operate its steel and tin finishing division at Fairless, with 850 workers. THE PHILADELPHIA INQUIRER/ MICHAEL VIOLA

continued to flourish, employing 6,000 workers in the 1920s. Fiorello La Guardia, Lyndon B. Johnson, and Tom Mix all wore Stetsons. So, on occasion, did Winston Churchill.

While Stetson was making hats in Kensington, Fayette R. Plumb was making tools in Frankford and Henry Disston was making saws in Tacony. Like Stetson hats, Disston saws and Plumb tools were known for quality across the country.

Perhaps the most flamboyant of Philadelphia's entrepreneurs was Peter A.B. Widener. A one-time butcher, he became city treasurer in a corrupt administration and in 1875 began acquiring trolley-line franchises. With William L. Elkins, he gained control of all the transit lines and went on to underwrite streetcar development in New York, Chicago, Pittsburgh, and Baltimore. He built great mansions, first on North Broad Street and later the 110-room Lynnewood Hall in Elkins Park. His son, George D. Widener, and grandson, Harry, went down with the Titanic in 1912. In their memory, the family established the Widener Library at Harvard University.

Edward T. Stotesbury, a Philadelphian of Quaker parents, served as a drummer boy in the Civil War and joined Drexel & Co., the Philadelphia investment house, in 1866. He worked there 72 years, until his death at 89 in 1938, heading it most of the time and becoming immensely wealthy. His crowning achievement was Whitemarsh Hall, an estate on 250 acres outside Chestnut Hill completed in 1922. With 145 rooms, 45 bathrooms and 14 elevators, it was the wonder of its day. After World War II, it was razed. Drexel & Co. likewise is no more.

On the northwest corner of City Hall stands a statue of Matthias William Baldwin, founder of the

**The Frankford Arsenal** provided work for tens of thousands. During World War II, 22,000 people worked around the clock, making 8 million rounds of ammunition a day. INQUIRER ARCHIVES / OEM DEFENSE PHOTO

Baldwin Locomotive Works. In its first 50 years, his factory at Broad and Spring Garden rolled out 5,000 steam engines — more than any other place on earth. Each bore the legend "Philadelphia, U.S.A." The company moved to Delaware County in 1928.

When William Cramp opened a small shipyard on the Delaware in 1830, there were a dozen shipyards. Cramp outdid them all by constructing speedy wooden clipper ships. When the Civil War brought the transition from wood to iron warships, William Cramp and Sons, now run by his son Charles, built the biggest ones afloat. It also built ocean liners, yachts, and American battleships. By 1895, its yard covered 32 acres and employed 6,000.

Shipbuilding generally slumped, but World War I brought a resurgence. The demand was so great that the nation's largest shipyard was built from scratch in 10 months on Hog Island, now the site of Philadelphia International Airport. Cramp shut down in 1927 but reopened in 1940 when the United States was rearming for World War II. During the war, employment at the Philadelphia Naval Shipyard peaked at 47,000 and the Delaware was again jammed with ships.

Since the closing of the Cramp yard in 1946, there has been little shipbuilding here. The collapse of this industry can serve as a metaphor for manufacturing generally in Philadelphia. The city that led the world in construction of ships, hats, and locomotives doesn't make them anymore. One by one, the bellwether companies of the first years of the 20th century have vanished. ∎

**Workers at Westinghouse Electric and Manufacturing Co.** in Lester, Delaware County, Pa., in 1927 are dwarfed by a casting weighing 36,000 pounds, part of a water intake system. INQUIRER ARCHIVES

**A large press stamps out a truck hood** at Budd Co.'s Hunting Park plant, which still produces car doors, fenders, and auto parts. Budd's Red Lion plant, which made railroad cars, closed in 1987. INQUIRER ARCHIVES / LAWRENCE S. WILLIAMS

**Heavy industry was a mainstay** of the city's manufacturing base, and Midvale Steel in Nicetown was a major employer. During World War II, Midvale workers turned out naval gun turrets and armor plate. This is a view of the Midvale yard, locomotives, and drivers in 1900. HAGLEY MUSEUM AND LIBRARY

**The Hog Island shipyard** has been called "the first great war boondoggle." It was hurriedly built in 1917, during wartime, on 947 acres of swampland along the Delaware, for which the U.S. government paid two prominent Philadelphians $2,000 an acre — double the estimated value. By the time the yard reached full production in late 1918, the war was over. Its peak production was in 1919 (shown here). The yard was closed in 1921, after launching 122 ships and a congressional investigation. In 1930 the city bought it for $3 million. It is now the site of Philadelphia International Airport. INQUIRER ARCHIVES / PHILADELPHIA MARITIME MUSEUM

**In the early years of aviation,** military planes were assembled at the Philadelphia Navy Yard. This 1936 photo shows assembly of Navy aircraft.

INQUIRER ARCHIVES / U.S. NAVY

**With a peak of 47,000 workers in the 1940s,** the Philadelphia Navy Yard (shown in 1919) was a bulwark of the local economy and a leader in naval technology. After nearly two centuries, the Navy closed the base. Sept. 15, 1995, was its last workday.

**General Electric operated a plant** in Southwest Philadelphia until the 1950s, when operations were moved to King of Prussia. Here, maintenance workers return to the job following a strike in 1946. THE PHILADELPHIA INQUIRER / ARTHUR DRESSLER

**The J.G. Brill Co.** was a major manufacturer of buses and streetcars. Founded by a German immigrant in 1869, the company grew and changed with evolving transit technology — producing cable cars, trolleys, electric streetcars, trackless trolleys, and, ultimately, buses at its West Philadelphia factory. THE PHILADELPHIA INQUIRER

**The Baldwin Locomotive Works,** at Broad and Spring Garden, was the nation's largest manufacturer of railroad steam engines. The company built locomotives in Philadelphia from 1832 until 1928, when it moved to Delaware County. The plant is shown in 1900.

FREE LIBRARY OF PHILADELPHIA / PRINT AND PICTURE COLLECTION

**It was not just heavy industry** that made Philadelphia the "Workshop of the World." Pharmaceuticals became a mainstay of the economy, with such major companies as Merck & Co., Wyeth-Ayerst, and SmithKline Beecham. In 1949, at what was then Smith Kline & French Laboratories, workers check machines in the tablet-coating operation.

THE PHILADELPHIA INQUIRER / RUSSELL SALMON

**A machine that would revolutionize the 20th-century workplace** was unveiled at the University of Pennsylvania Feb. 14, 1946. It was 80 feet long, weighed 30 tons, and contained 18,000 vacuum tubes. ENIAC — short for Electronic Numerical Integrator and Calculator — launched the computer age. It was the forerunner of Univac, the first electronic computer for commercial use.

UNIVERSITY OF PENNSYLVANIA ARCHIVES

**The Disston Saw Co.** in Tacony was famous for the quality of its products. Workers in 1910 are using hand files to finish individual saw blades.

**Stetson — the brand worn by Tom Mix, Fiorello La Guardia and Lyndon B. Johnson** — was a famous Philadelphia hatmaker, established in 1865 and long located at Fifth Street and Montgomery Avenue. John B. Stetson's company employed 6,000 people in the 1920s. Hats were tied on wooden blocks, ironed, then finished by hand, as this worker is doing in 1948. INQUIRER ARCHIVES / PHOTO-ILLUSTRATORS

**Women and girls were heavily employed** in the textile and clothing industries. In this 1918 photo, a Philadelphia girl winds silk yarn, used in weaving and knitting, at Sauquoit Silk Manufacturing Co., located on Clarissa Street just below Wayne Junction.

PENNSYLVANIA STATE ARCHIVES / PHILADELPHIA COMMERCIAL MUSEUM COLLECTION

**The garment and needletrades industries** employed tens of thousands of people in the northeastern United States in the early years of the century. Workers at the Woodbine Children's Clothing Co. in Woodbine, N.J., pause for a photo in 1910.

**Philadelphia has been a publishing center since the days of Ben Franklin.** Book publishers, such as Lippincott's, thrived here, but the main source of mass entertainment before TV was the general-interest magazine. Curtis Publishing Co. dominated the field, with *Ladies' Home Journal*, *Farm Journal*, and the *Saturday Evening Post*. This is the composing room in 1918, when 3,000 people were employed at the Curtis Building, Sixth and Walnut, facing Independence Square. PENNSYLVANIA STATE ARCHIVES / PHILADELPHIA COMMERCIAL MUSEUM COLLECTION

**Workers at the Christian Schmidt Brewing Co.,** at Second and Girard, load beer kegs circa 1940. Schmidt, a German immigrant, opened his brewery in 1860 and was selling 100,000 barrels a year by 1892. At the turn of the century, around 90 breweries flourished here. Schmidt's, which closed in 1987, was the last to go, joining such local brews as Ortlieb, Engels & Wolf, and Esslinger.

BALCH INSTITUTE FOR ETHNIC STUDIES LIBRARY / SCHMIDT AND SONS COLLECTION

**Hardwick and Magee,** at Seventh and Lehigh in North Philadelphia, was a nationally recognized maker of carpets, dating to 1837. The company produced an innovative seamed rug and became famous for these colorfully floral-patterned carpets, used in hotels, restaurants, and theaters. Non-union competition from companies in the South and synthetic rugs led to its bankruptcy in 1972. This 1918 photo shows the company's "designer's row."

PENNSYLVANIA STATE ARCHIVES /
PHILADELPHIA COMMERCIAL MUSEUM COLLECTION

**Household appliances — radios, TV sets, refrigerators, irons, toasters** — were in big demand after World War II, when production resumed. In this 1947 photo, workers at Proctor Electric Co. inspect and pack irons. The company, whose parent firm was founded in Philadelphia, later merged with Silex and in 1978 moved to King of Prussia. It was acquired by Wesray Corp. in 1983 and moved to Chillicothe, Ohio. The company manufactures toasters, irons, and coffeemakers. INQUIRER ARCHIVES

**Philadelphia was an early center of the television industry,** and Philco (shown in 1948) was once the city's largest peacetime employer. Another local company, Jerrold Electronics, founded by future governor Milton Shapp at 15th and Lehigh, was the world's leading maker of amplified antenna systems to beam TV to remote areas. INQUIRER ARCHIVES

**For many years, Exide Battery** had a plant at Adams and Rising Sun Avenues. It was shuttered in 1978 and a shopping center opened on the old factory site. The Exide Corp. is now based in Reading. This shot was taken in 1958. THE PHILADELPHIA INQUIRER

**Workers at the Consolidated Dressed Beef Co.** in 1931 move sides of beef into coolers, before quartering them for shipment. The city's meat-packing center was on the east bank of the Schuylkill at 36th Street and Grays Ferry Avenue. THE PHILADELPHIA INQUIRER

**At Nabisco's plant on Roosevelt Boulevard at Byberry Road** in the Northeast, David Sine inspects a parade of passing crackers in 1988. The plant now employs about 885 people, making Oreos, Ritz crackers, and other snacks.

THE PHILADELPHIA INQUIRER / WILLIAM F. STEINMETZ

**Whitman's chocolates** were made at 9701 Roosevelt Boulevard until 1993. The plant, shown in 1984, closed after Whitman's parent company was sold.

THE PHILADELPHIA INQUIRER / SARAH LEEN

**Mrs. Paul's Kitchens was founded in 1946** by entrepreneur Edward J. Piszek and the Roxborough company became famous for fish sticks, one of the early frozen foods. Since Piszek sold in 1982 to Campbell Soup, ownership has changed hands three times. The fish sticks are now made by Aurora Foods Inc. in San Francisco.

THE PHILADELPHIA INQUIRER / WILLIAM F. STEINMETZ

# Culture and Society

DURING THE GREAT DEPRESSION, when bread lines twisted down South Street, conductor Leopold Stokowski could be seen tooling around town in his silvery three-wheeled Dymaxion car, the aerodynamic invention of designer and thinker R. Buckminster Fuller.

The image of Stokowski behind the wheel of Fuller's quirky car speaks volumes about art, culture and society in 20th-century Philadelphia. Perhaps more than in any other city, cultural life here has been the product of a sometimes improbable tension between complacency and insurgency, parochialism and romance.

**A 1982 postage stamp** honors Philadelphia-born John, Ethel, and Lionel Barrymore.
© U.S. POSTAL SERVICE.

The Philadelphia Orchestra, founded precisely at the turn of the century, has been an instrument of social prestige since the beginning. Supported by the quiet old money of the Main Line, the orchestra and its hall — the venerable Academy of Music — served as social headquarters for elite Philadelphia, which Christopher Morley described in 1920 as a "large town at the confluence of the Biddle and the Drexel families ... surrounded by cricket teams, fox hunters, beagle packs and the Pennsylvania Railroad."

Yet as an artistic institution, the orchestra achieved world renown under the flamboyant Stokowski, who became music director in 1912 and promptly began introducing the innovative sounds of such composers as Igor Stravinsky and Alban Berg. But even the great Stokowski could not withstand the disapproving clucks of local audi-

**The ornate Academy of Music** has been the center of Philadelphia's musical life since it opened in 1857. THE PHILADELPHIA INQUIRER

ences. He quit after innumerable disagreements over the orchestra's repertoire, and was replaced in 1937 by Eugene Ormandy, a man of more conservative tastes.

Through a happy coincidence of timing, the orchestra was coming of age at the same time as radio, and Philadelphia – with such local companies as A. Atwater Kent, Philco and RCA Victor ("His Master's Voice") – became a center of radio manufacturing and broadcasting. Stokowski and Ormandy pushed the orchestra onto the world stage through a series of technological firsts: the first symphonic orchestra to make electrical recordings (1925, at RCA in Camden); the first to have a commercially sponsored radio broadcast (1929, on NBC); the first to perform on a film soundtrack (Paramount's *The Big Broadcast of 1937*); the first to appear in an animated film (Walt Disney's *Fantasia*, 1939); the first on a national TV broadcast (on CBS in 1948). And in 1997, the orchestra became the first to perform live on the Internet.

**The Pennsylvania Ballet** presents such star performers as Tamara Hadley and Bill DeGregory, here rehearsing *Coppelia* in 1986.

THE PHILADELPHIA INQUIRER / RON TARVER

Opera and theater in Philadelphia have revolved more around stars than enduring institutions, with the city regularly producing great voices. But in 1908, Oscar Hammerstein discovered Philadelphians wouldn't travel north of Market Street to hear even the greatest singers after he opened the Metropolitan Opera House at Broad and Poplar. It closed in 1910. Opera lovers flocked to the New York Metropolitan Opera, which played regularly in Philadelphia, and they swarmed to hear Enrico Caruso, who spent long periods in Philadelphia both performing and recording at the RCA studios. South Philadelphia's Mario Lanza – who never sang on the stage at all – celebrated Caruso in *The Great Caruso* (MGM, 1951).

West Chester-born composer Samuel Barber saw Caruso in New York, which inspired him to write an opera (set in Chester County) at age 7. Barber went on, in 1924, to the Curtis Institute of Music, where he studied with Fritz Reiner and became a friend of Gian-Carlo Menotti's.

Personalities have ruled theater in Philadelphia as well. Edwin Forrest dominated the 19th century and the Drew-Barrymore family dominated the 20th. Lionel, Ethel, and John Barrymore grew up in the home of their grandmother, Louisa Lane Drew, actress and manager of the Arch Street Theatre. Yet the stage play most closely identified with the city was written by a non-native, Philip Barry, who recreated Main Line society in his hit play, *The Philadelphia Story* (1939). Bryn Mawr grad Katharine Hepburn starred in the Hollywood version (1940), playing a role modeled on socialite Hope Montgomery Scott.

The clubby, complacent Philadelphia that outraged muckraker Lincoln Steffens and caused native son W.C. Fields to make jokes about his hometown provided the financial support and stability for its cultural institutions. But it drove a lot of talent away. The list of those who fled, either to escape the claustrophobic culture or to take advantage of opportunity in New York or Europe, includes opera stars Marian Anderson and Anna Moffo, artist Man Ray, playwright Charles Fuller, poets Ezra Pound and Hilda Doolittle, and artist Mary Cassatt (sister of a president of the Pennsylvania Railroad).

But the list of those who stayed is illustrious, too. Illustrator N.C. Wyeth of Chadds Ford loved the Brandywine area. So do his son, Andrew, and grandson, Jamie. From Frank Furness to Louis Kahn, Robert Venturi and Denise Scott-Brown, Philadelphia has been home to some of the nation's greatest architects. Albert C. Barnes also stayed, but after an exhibit of his art collection at the Pennsylvania Academy was panned in 1923, he took his treasures to Merion and restricted who could see them.

Then there was Bucky Fuller. He found a home for his projects at the University City Science Center in the 1970s. By then, he had moved from the Dymaxion car to the geodesic dome. Stokowski was long gone. And so was most of the stodginess so cherished by city fathers a century ago. ∎

. . . . . . . . . . . . . . . . . . . . . . . . . . . . . . . . . . . . . . . . . . . . . . . .

**The Union League,** bastion of Philadelphia business and society, began as a Republican political club during the Civil War. It came to symbolize a tight group of socially prominent businessmen.

THE PHILADELPHIA INQUIRER

**Four generations of Philadelphia Orchestra conductors: Fritz Scheel** was the founding music director in 1900. Leopold Stokowski took over in 1912. His successor was Eugene Ormandy, who took the baton in 1937, followed by Riccardo Muti in 1980.

**Leopold Stokowski** assembled a group of out-of-work musicians for a concert during the Depression in 1932 and later directed them in a benefit for needy musicians.

**Riccardo Muti's** tenure ended in 1992; he was succeeded by Wolfgang Sawallisch.

**Eugene Ormandy**
conducts the
orchestra in 1930.

**Enrico Caruso,** front left, spent much time in Philadelphia in the early years of the century, singing with the Metropolitan Opera and recording at the RCA studios in Camden, N.J. INQUIRER ARCHIVES

**After an international singing and movie career, Paul Robeson** was labeled a Communist and his passport was revoked in 1950. He moved to Philadelphia to live with a sister and died here in 1976.

INQUIRER ARCHIVES / ARTS MANAGEMENT CORP.

**Long the symbol of RCA Victor records,** an image of Nipper listening to a recording of "His Master's Voice" on a Victrola adorns a stained glass window on the Victor building at Market Street and Delaware Avenue in Camden. The tower was converted to luxury apartments.

PHILADELPHIA DAILY NEWS / ALEJANDRO A. ALVAREZ

**One of the great cultural scandals** of the century occurred in 1939, when the Daughters of the American Revolution refused to allow contralto Marian Anderson of Philadelphia to sing at Constitution Hall in Washington because of her race. Amid the public outrage, Eleanor Roosevelt resigned from the DAR and arranged for her to perform instead at the Lincoln Memorial, where there was a massive turnout.

UNIVERSITY OF PENNSYLVANIA / ANNENBERG RARE BOOK & MANUSCRIPT LIBRARY

**Before Anna Moffo became a star of the Metropolitan Opera,** Philadelphians could hear her for free at the Curtis Institute of Music's student concerts. Moffo, who grew up in Wayne and was valedictorian of her Radnor High School class, was a regular on the Paoli Local in the 1950s, when she commuted to Curtis. Here, the soprano takes a bow at a 1973 *Evening at the Pops* concert on PBS. INQUIRER ARCHIVES / PBS

**Composer Samuel Barber,** born in West Chester, attended the newly formed Curtis Institute of Music starting in 1924, when he was 14. There Barber met Gian-Carlo Menotti, and the two became friends for life. Here, Barber (center), who twice won the Pulitzer Prize, poses in 1936 in Rome with the Curtis String Quartet, (from left) Orlando Cole, Jascha Brodsky, Max Aronoff, and Charles Joffe. INQUIRER ARCHIVES

**South Philadelphia's Mario Lanza** was an operatic singer who never made his living on the stage. Instead, he went to Hollywood and made a half-dozen movies between 1949 and 1959, when he died at 38. His most popular role was *The Great Caruso*. Lanza was born in a house at Sixth and Christian Streets. In 1952, he was photographed singing for Rafaella Fasano, a polio victim from New Jersey.

MARIO LANZA INSTITUTE AND MUSEUM

**Alexander Calder,** grandson of the sculptor of the City Hall statues, invented the mobile, one of which hangs over the grand staircase in the Philadelphia Museum of Art. THE PHILADELPHIA INQUIRER

**Three generations of Calders** have enriched the city: Alexander Milne Calder (left, 1900), creator of the William Penn statue atop City Hall and its other sculptures; his son, Alexander Stirling Calder, designer of Swann Fountain on Logan Circle; and his grandson, Alexander Calder, whose mobiles grace the Art Museum.

**Alexander Stirling Calder** works on a sculpture in 1923.

**Andrew Wyeth's son, Jamie,** continues the realist tradition into the third generation.

THE PHILADELPHIA INQUIRER / BEVERLY SCHAEFER

**The Rodin Museum on the Parkway,** with *The Thinker*, was dedicated in 1929. The museum was made possible through the generosity of theater impresario Jules Mastbaum. At the dedication were (from left) Mrs. Harry Mackey, wife of the mayor; Rene Claudel; Mayor Mackey; Mayor James J. Walker of New York; Mrs. Jules Mastbaum; French Ambassador Paul Claudel. INQUIRER ARCHIVES / UNIVERSAL NEWSREEL PHOTO

**Another famous art dynasty,**
the Wyeths, began with
grandfather N.C. Wyeth (at left),
who was an illustrator and
founder of the Brandywine
school of painting in the early
years of the century.

**Andrew Wyeth,** son of N.C. Wyeth, created popular
paintings of the Chester County countryside.
Born in 1917, he grew up in Chadds Ford and
still lives there, summering in Maine. During the
1980s, the art world clucked over his relationship
with his Chadds Ford neighbor, Helga Testorff,
model for the "Helga paintings."

**Henry Ossawa Tanner,** who studied with Thomas Eakins at the Pennsylvania Academy of the Fine Arts, left for Paris as a young man and never returned. The photo was taken in his studio about 1935. INQUIRER ARCHIVES / SMITHSONIAN INSTITUTION

**Fiske Kimball,** director of the Philadelphia Museum of Art from 1925 to 1955, is credited with turning a minor collection into a first-rate museum. When it opened March 26, 1928, he had to scramble to fill the galleries. In 1954, he and Mrs. George D. Beck admire a Giorgio de Chirico painting. THE PHILADELPHIA INQUIRER / JOHN CULROSS

**The Neoclassical home of the Philadelphia Museum of Art** opened in 1928, during the long tenure of director Fiske Kimball, who greatly expanded the collections. The current chief executive is Anne d'Harnoncourt, photographed in 1982 with art patron Robert Montgomery Scott, then the museum's president. THE PHILADELPHIA INQUIRER / AKIRA SUWA

**Attorney John G. Johnson** in 1917 gave the Philadelphia Museum of Art his paintings and art objects, which form the core of its early European collection.

INQUIRER ARCHIVES / PHILADELPHIA MUSEUM OF ART

**Albert Barnes,** an early collector of impressionist and post-impressionist paintings, turned his back on the art establishment after it snubbed him, creating his own institution in Merion with only limited public access. Barnes cultivated African-American artists, such as Horace Pippin, shown here in 1944. Interest in the Barnes Foundation soared after 80 of the paintings were exhibited abroad from 1993 to '95. TEMPLE UNIVERSITY / CHARLES L. BLOCKSON COLLECTION, JOHN W. MOSLEY

**Charles L. Blockson** is one of the nation's foremost collectors of African-American artifacts and books. Almost no research on African-American history and culture can be complete without consulting his collections, housed at Temple University. THE PHILADELPHIA INQUIRER / SHARON J. WOHLMUTH

**Henry McIlhenny,** photographed in 1983 at his home in Center City, donated his entire collection of paintings and artifacts to the Philadelphia Museum of Art when he died in 1986. His collection of paintings was valued at more than $50 million. THE PHILADELPHIA INQUIRER / AKIRA SUWA

**The Philadelphia Story:** The role of socialite Tracy Lord, portrayed by Bryn Mawr grad Katharine Hepburn in the movie *The Philadelphia Story*, was based on the life of Hope Montgomery Scott of Radnor. Hope and Edgar Scott's farm, Ardrossan, was one of the last great Main Line estates. Since their deaths in 1995, the farm has been subdivided for luxury homes. THE PHILADELPHIA INQUIRER / ROBERT L. MOONEY

**In the days when Society mattered,** everybody who was anybody attended the Assembly, the annual ball at the Bellevue Stratford. It was said that couples stayed together because they wouldn't be invited to the Assembly if divorced. TEMPLE URBAN ARCHIVES / THE EVENING BULLETIN

**Financier Anthony J. Drexel Jr.,** grandson of the founder of Drexel University, was a cohort of J.P. Morgan's. Part of their century-old investment banking empire crashed when Drexel Burnham Lambert collapsed in the junk-bond scandal of the 1980s. INQUIRER ARCHIVES

**Novelist Pearl Buck,** who once lived on the 2000 block of Delancey Place, was presented the Nobel Prize by King Gustav of Sweden in 1938 for *The Good Earth* and other writings about Chinese life. Out of concern for millions of children orphaned by World War II, she founded the Pearl Buck Foundation in Bucks County, which arranges international adoptions. INQUIRER ARCHIVES / ASSOCIATED PRESS

**Bucks County's James Michener** won the 1948 Pulitzer Prize for his collection of stories, *Tales of the South Pacific*. One of America's most prolific authors, Michener also founded the James A. Michener Museum of Art in Doylestown.

THE PHILADELPHIA INQUIRER

**Playwright Charles Fuller won the Pulitzer Prize** in 1982 for *A Soldier's Play*, presented in New York that year by the Negro Ensemble Company.

THE PHILADELPHIA INQUIRER / REBECCA BARGER

**Literary Philadelphia** owes much of its stolidly middle-class reputation in the first half of the century to the presence here of Curtis Publishing Company's *Saturday Evening Post* and *Ladies' Home Journal*.

FREE LIBRARY OF PHILADELPHIA

**Philadelphia's genteel tradition** was chronicled by Christopher Morley.

INQUIRER ARCHIVES

**E. Digby Baltzell, a University of Pennsylvania sociologist,** coined the term "WASP" (white Anglo-Saxon Protestant) and made a career of it. In *The Protestant Establishment*, *Philadelphia Gentlemen*, and *Puritan Boston and Quaker Philadelphia*, he wrote about social class and elites.

THE PHILADELPHIA INQUIRER / KENDALL WILKINSON

**The geodesic dome** was the most famous creation of R. Buckminster Fuller, one of the city's great thinkers and designers.
He used the University City Science Center as a base for research and gabfests. INQUIRER ARCHIVES

**Louis Kahn,** one of America's greatest 20th-century architects, lived in Philadelphia most of his life and taught architecture at the University of Pennsylvania, where one of his most famous buildings is located. The Alfred Newton Richards Medical and Biological Laboratories was completed in 1965. THE PHILADELPHIA INQUIRER / RUSSELL SALMON

**Husband-and-wife team Robert Venturi and Denise Scott-Brown** are the city's most influential contemporary architects. Their work includes Franklin Court, Guild House, and Welcome Park on Second Street. PHILADELPHIA DAILY NEWS / KENNETH F. IRBY

# Movers
# and Shakers

APRIL 5, 1968: AFTER THE ASSASSINATION of the Rev. Dr. Martin Luther King Jr., America faced the threat of widespread rioting. In Philadelphia, R. Stewart Rauch Jr. met with Richard C. Bond and William L. Day — the pinnacle of the Philadelphia Establishment. Rauch was head of the Philadelphia Saving Fund Society, Bond was president of Wanamakers, Day was chairman of First Pennsylvania Bank.

Chicago and Washington had already exploded in rioting. Philadelphia might be next. The trio began working the phones. Before that day was out, they had raised $1 million to create an agency that evolved into the Philadelphia Urban Coalition. The city kept the lid on. "I had never seen anything like it," said W. Thacher Longstreth, who then headed the Chamber of Commerce.

**Rudolph Blankenburg,** reform mayor, defeated the GOP machine in 1910.
INQUIRER ARCHIVES

Such forceful action by the city's movers and shakers was comparatively rare then. It still is. But if the Quaker City has gained a reputation for complacency, it also has nurtured hundreds of brilliant men and women who typify Philadelphia's special brand of quiet achievement.

Some are better known than others. Maggie Kuhn made the Gray Panthers into a national force. Sociologist Digby Baltzell coined the term "WASP." The American Friends Service Committee carried Quaker principles around the

**Republican Thacher Longstreth and Democrat Frank Rizzo** examine socks at the airport in 1984. Argyle socks were Longstreth's trademark. THE PHILADELPHIA INQUIRER / VICKI VALERIO

world. Mother Katherine Drexel moved closer to sainthood.

Baruch Blumberg won a Nobel Prize for cancer research and Lawrence Klein won one in the field of economics. Frank N. Piasecki pioneered in the development of helicopters and Dr. John H. Gibbon Jr. developed the heart-lung machine. C. Everett Koop, as U.S. surgeon general, alerted the nation to the perils of cigarette smoking. A. Leon Higginbotham wrote eloquently about the issue that W.E.B. DuBois defined in 1903: "The problem of the 20th century is the problem of the color line."

America's most innovative retailer, John Wanamaker, opened his flagship department store across from City Hall in 1911. Filmmaker Steven Spielberg, who grew up in Haddon-field, has childhood memories of gazing at the giant bronze eagle and towering pipe organs in Wanamakers' grand court.

Displays of raw power are out of character in Philadelphia, and maybe that's just as well. In the early years of the century, Boies Penrose, scion of one of the city's richest and most distinguished colonial families, proved to be a corrupt and devious political boss. Penrose dominated Philadelphia's politics from 1904 until his death in 1921.

William S. Vare, who seized control on the death of Penrose, drew his power from the slum wards of Center City and the immigrant rowhouses of South Philadelphia. Much of the money that kept his machine well oiled came from the Vare Construction Co., which won huge contracts from companies wishing to ingratiate themselves with the city's boss. Vare's career ended ignominiously. He won election to the U.S. Senate in 1928 but was denied his seat for excessive campaign spending.

Philadelphia was controlled by Republicans for 67 years, until liberal Democrats Joseph S. Clark and Richardson Dilworth ended the GOP's long run in 1951. With Clark as mayor and Dilworth as district attorney, the city government, which had been wracked with scandal, entered a reform period that attracted national attention. Its planning director, Edmund N. Bacon, was a mover in his own right, his bold projects gaining him recognition on the cover of *Time* in 1964. Clark left after one term for a U.S. Senate seat but Dilworth, a charismatic leader, succeeded him as mayor.

**G. Stockton Strawbridge,** grandson of a founder of Strawbridge & Clothier, spearheaded the resurgence of Market Street. INQUIRER ARCHIVES

Dilworth inspired strong loyalties. And so did his nemesis, Frank L. Rizzo, the policeman's son from South Philly who rose to become police commissioner and serve two terms as mayor (1972-80). Dilworth and Rizzo came from different social classes and despised each other. The stereo-typical Philadelphian is said to be self-effacing and soft-spoken. These two broke the mold. Like Dilworth, Rizzo, the first Italian American to head the police department and the city's first Italian-American mayor, delighted in controversy. And his years in power were filled with it.

When an ex-Marine named Cecil B. Moore entered politics in Philadelphia in the 1950s, the black presence was negligible. Moore, a defense lawyer, was determined to change that, and he did. Brash, profane and combative, he took over the local NAACP and launched a campaign to integrate all-white labor unions. He led the successful drive to integrate Girard College. In 1963, he became the first black candidate for mayor.

Leon H. Sullivan, longtime pastor of Zion Baptist Church in North Philadelphia, was known as the "Lion of Zion," for his extraordinary leadership as a churchman and civic leader. In 1964, he launched a self-help program that he called Opportunities Industrialization Center. OIC spread about the country and around the world. More than three million people are said to have received job training at its centers. In 1968, Sullivan started Progress Plaza in North Philadelphia, the city's first black-owned and black-operated shopping center.

In recent years, much of the private sector's moving and shaking was supplied by developer Willard Rouse 3rd, who successfully challenged the unwritten ban against buildings taller than City Hall by erecting Liberty Place in 1989. His 60-floor skyscraper transformed Center City both physically and psychologically.

In city government, the chief mover and shaker for eight years, through 1999, was Mayor Edward G. Rendell, whose administration rescued Philadelphia from near bankruptcy and set it on the path to solvency. Perhaps most important, Rendell, a transplanted New Yorker, got Philadelphians to believe in themselves and in their city. Thanks in part to his ministrations, Center City throbbed with life as the century neared its close. ■

**William S. Vare,** with his daughters in 1926, was one of a string of Republican bosses who ruled Philadelphia in the first half of the century. The political base of the three Vare brothers — George, Edwin, and William — was South Philly. THE PHILADELPHIA INQUIRER

**Albert M. Greenfield's bank** failed in the Depression, but he recovered to become a major figure after World War II. His company owned the Bellevue Stratford, Lit Brothers, and Yellow Cab. In 1948, he helped bring two national conventions to town.

HISTORICAL SOCIETY OF
PENNSYLVANIA

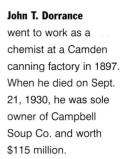

**John T. Dorrance** went to work as a chemist at a Camden canning factory in 1897. When he died on Sept. 21, 1930, he was sole owner of Campbell Soup Co. and worth $115 million.

HISTORICAL SOCIETY
OF PENNSYLVANIA

**Joseph Newton Pew** in 1886 founded the Sun Oil Co., now Sunoco Inc., based in Philadelphia. Pew and his four children established the Pew Charitable Trusts, a Philadelphia philanthropy that gave away $213 million in 1998. INQUIRER ARCHIVES

**Boies Penrose,** scion of one of the city's oldest, richest, and most distinguished colonial families, proved to be a corrupt and devious boss. A U.S. senator, he dominated Philadelphia's politics from 1904 until his death in 1921. Penrose ran for mayor in 1895 but lost the primary, thanks to a well-publicized photo of him coming out of a brothel.

In 1951, liberal Democrats Joseph S. Clark (left) and Richardson Dilworth broke 67 years of GOP control. With Clark as mayor and Dilworth as district attorney, city government entered a reform period. Clark served from 1952 to '56 and was succeeded by Dilworth. THE PHILADELPHIA INQUIRER

Philadelphian Hugh Scott represented Pennsylvania in Congress for 40 years, the last 18 in the Senate. As Senate Republican leader from 1969 to '77, Scott wielded enormous influence. He died at 93 in 1994. THE PHILADELPHIA INQUIRER

Walter Annenberg inherited *The Philadelphia Inquirer* from his father, who bought the paper in 1936. Annenberg's Triangle Publications owned *TV Guide*, the *Daily Racing Form*, and TV and radio stations. After being named ambassador to the Court of St. James's by President Nixon in 1969, Annenberg sold the paper to Knight Newspapers, now Knight Ridder Inc.

INQUIRER ARCHIVES

In a famous 1969 photograph, Police Commissioner Frank Rizzo arrives at a crime scene in South Philadelphia from a formal dinner party with a nightstick tucked in his waistband.

**Raymond Pace Alexander and his wife, Sadie,** were early leaders of the African-American community. Both lawyers, she served as assistant city solicitor from 1928 to '30; he served on City Council during the Clark-Dilworth reform period in the 1950s.
THE PHILADELPHIA INQUIRER / JOSEPH COLEMAN

**A. Leon Higginbotham** was the first African American to head a federal regulatory agency, the Federal Trade Commission, in 1962. Over the resistance of a Mississippi senator, he was confirmed and served as a U.S. District Court judge in Philadelphia from 1964 to '77, and as judge, chief judge, and senior judge of the Third Circuit from 1977 to '93. He went on to teach at Harvard and write about slavery in colonial America. He died in 1998. THE PHILADELPHIA INQUIRER / JOHN COSTELLO

In 1968, the Rev. Leon H. Sullivan, longtime pastor of Zion Baptist Church, started Progress Plaza, the city's first black-owned and black-operated shopping center, at Broad and Oxford in North Philadelphia. He is shown at the center's dedication. Nationally, he is best known as author of the Sullivan Principles, a set of standards for corporations that sought to do business with apartheid South Africa.

THE PHILADELPHIA INQUIRER / MICHAEL VIOLA

**Mary Patterson McPherson** presided over Bryn Mawr College for 18 years, from 1978 to 1997, when she joined the Mellon Foundation. Midway through her presidency, she questioned whether women's colleges would survive and began establishing academic collaborations with Haverford, Swarthmore, and Penn.

THE PHILADELPHIA INQUIRER / SHARON J. WOHLMUTH

**Quaker leader Asia Bennett** in 1980 became the first woman to head the American Friends Service Committee, an organization of Quaker volunteers and relief workers. She served as executive secretary of the committee, based at 15th and Cherry Streets, from 1980 to 1992. "A quiet, smiling presence" is how she was described by Quaker historian Margaret Bacon. PHILADELPHIA DAILY NEWS / SUSAN WINTERS

The first black woman City Council member, **Ethel Allen** cracked the city's power structure three ways: as a black, as a woman, and as a Republican. She gave up a medical practice in 1971 to win a Council seat. Allen tackled the volatile issue of gang warfare in the 1970s. She died of a heart attack in 1981, at age 52.

THE PHILADELPHIA INQUIRER / JOSEPH T. MARTIN

**Judge Lisa Richette,** who has served for 28 years on the Common Pleas bench, is known as an avowed liberal, an anti-war activist, a feminist, and an advocate for at-risk children and the homeless. She has been called a "limousine liberal," a "mollycoddler," and "Let-'em-Loose Lisa," the latter by Frank Rizzo in an election effort to unseat her. Richette wound up the top vote-getter. THE PHILADELPHIA INQUIRER / JAMES G. DOMKE

**Taking the seat of power in 1984, W. Wilson Goode** became the city's first black mayor. As city managing director under Mayor Bill Green, Goode gained a reputation as an effective and hard-working administrator. He served two terms as mayor but his tenure was forever scarred by the bombing of the MOVE house in 1985. PHILADELPHIA DAILY NEWS / E.W. FAIRCLOTH

**A preacher's son, the Rev. William H. Gray 3rd** played a dual role: as longtime pastor of Bright Hope Baptist Church in North Philadelphia and as an influential member of Congress, 1979-91. Gray left Congress to become president of the United Negro College Fund.

THE PHILADELPHIA INQUIRER / JOHN COSTELLO

Philadelphia was close to bankruptcy in 1991 when Edward G. Rendell won election as mayor. He set the city on the path to solvency. On election night in 1991, he is joined by his son, Jesse (right), and his wife, Marjorie. He was elected governor of Pennsylvania in 2002. THE PHILADELPHIA INQUIRER / ED HILLE

Republican Arlen Specter, a former Philadelphia D.A., was elected to the U.S. Senate in 1980. Specter became nationally known for his "single-bullet theory" in the John F. Kennedy assassination while serving on the Warren Commission. Elected to his fifth term in 2004, he is shown with his wife, Joan, on election night 1986.

THE PHILADELPHIA INQUIRER / JOHN COSTELLO

# The War Years

WAR FOR AMERICANS in the 20th century was always "over there" — in Europe, in Asia, on the islands of the Pacific or the sands of the Middle East (though occasionally submarines raided within sight of the Jersey coast). Even so, the wars reached deep into nearly every Philadelphia household.

The European war that began in August 1914 seemed at first to be no business of the United States. Philadelphia, with its heritage of Quaker pacifism and its immigrants from all the combatant countries, embraced the national policy of neutrality.

But sentiment soon shifted against Germany, after it invaded Belgium and began unrestricted submarine warfare. When the passenger liner Lusitania was torpedoed in May 1915, among the 128 Americans who died were 27 Philadelphians, including Paul Crompton's entire family of eight.

When the United States entered the war in April 1917, the city signed on with zeal. The Pennsylvania National Guard — one quarter of its troops Philadelphians — was federalized as the 28th, or "Iron Division," its emblem a keystone. After the draft began in June 1917, many of the 53,000 Philadelphians inducted went into the 79th Division. Both units saw heavy fighting in France. Women joined, too — 2,000 from the city served.

**Exuberant servicemen and civilians celebrate VJ Day**
(Victory over Japan) in Philadelphia on Aug. 14, 1945.
The war, at last, was over. THE PHILADELPHIA INQUIRER

At home, the demands of war dominated the "Workshop of the World," as Philadelphia factories began supplying virtually every need: helmets, saddles, knives, locomotives. And ships. In addition to the shipyards already operating from Chester to Bristol, the Emergency Fleet Corp. took 947 acres of marshy ground south of the city — part of the present airport — and built the sprawling Hog Island yard.

The winter of 1917-18 was so cold that Hog Island's builders had to use steam lines to thaw the ground so it could be broken up with jackhammers. In city stores and offices, Heatless Mondays were observed to conserve coal. There were Wheatless Mondays and Wednesdays as well — no flour — and families turned any open space into "victory gardens." They contributed more directly to the war effort through Liberty Loan drives, buying bonds at rallies, sing-alongs, and the new motion-picture houses.

Patriotism sometimes went overboard: The school board prohibited the teaching of German. Sauerkraut was redubbed "Liberty cabbage."

The war's end in November 1918 brought jubilation, and renewed determination to be free of Europe's conflicts. Thousands turned out to welcome the troop ships home.

Philadelphia was a changing city in the 1920s; immigration continued to swell the population of the nation's third-largest city. But when the Cramp's shipyard announced that no new ships would slide down the ways, the long erosion of the city's industrial base began.

The situation worsened with the Depression of the 1930s. When, by 1940, it became clear that a new war was inevitable, industry once again began gearing up.

Isolationist sentiment was still strong, but it was blown away forever by the surprise Japanese air attack on the U.S. Pacific fleet at Pearl Harbor, Hawaii, on Dec. 7, 1941. Even before the attack, the draft had been reinstituted and the 28th Division again was inducted into federal service. By the end of World War II, more than 183,000 Philadelphians would be in the service.

But this time, those left behind couldn't be sure that war wouldn't come to them. London had been bombed, and suddenly a mere ocean seemed no guarantee of safety. Air-raid drills and blackouts became regular occurrences. Many basic commodities — meat, sugar, rubber, gasoline — were rationed.

The Baldwin Locomotive Works began turning out tanks; the Cramp shipyard reopened. When able-bodied men grew scarce, companies recruited women on a scale that was to alter the rhythms of family life irrevocably.

Many homes put small banners in the windows with a blue star for each family member in service. The star became gold when a loved one wasn't coming back.

The war-weary city celebrated Victory in Europe Day on May 8, 1945, and had a two-day blowout after Japan stopped fighting on Aug. 14. Japan had not quit, though, until two atomic bombs had been dropped on her cities.

But the bomb did not engender true peace. The Soviet Union, so recently an ally, and later the communist government of China became America's new adversaries. In Korea, the communist government of the North invaded the U.S.-allied South in June 1950. American troops, under the flag of the United Nations, fought in a war that ended in stalemate in July 1953, at a cost of 54,246 U.S. lives.

In Southeast Asia, the Vietnam War likewise was seen as an effort to repel communist expansionism. The first U.S. ground troops were committed in 1965. But as the war dragged on, many questioned the American role. The draft became a divisive issue, as working-class young men were picked to go and risk their lives, while college boys were spared through deferments.

This time, there was no closing of ranks in Philadelphia, or elsewhere. For the families of 66 young men from Thomas Edison High School in North Philadelphia, it was devastating. That was the war's toll from that one school — reportedly the highest of any public school in the country. ■

**As a train pulls out,** mothers and wives weep for draftees in the 79th Division, heading for basic training at Camp Meade, Md. Drafting of troops began in June 1917. STANLEY CO. OF AMERICA

**Doughboys line up to board trains** in Philadelphia. By war's end, about 90,000 from the city had served. THE LIBRARY COMPANY OF PHILADELPHIA

QUISTCONCK

QUISTCONCK

QUISTCONCK
HULL A 492
YARD
1

**Troops of the 28th Division** — Pennsylvania's "Iron Division" — enjoy an impromptu musical show amid the wreckage of the town of Thiaucourt in northeast France, which fell to U.S. forces in September 1918. The former Pennsylvania National Guard unit was federalized in July 1917.

INQUIRER ARCHIVES

**President Woodrow Wilson** and his wife, Edith (in white on platform), launch Hog Island's first ship, the Quistconck, on Aug. 5, 1918. The 947-acre yard, where the airport is now located, was built in a matter of months after the United States entered the war.

INQUIRER ARCHIVES / SUN SHIPBUILDING & DRY DOCK CO.

**Pennsylvania men of the 28th Division** arrive home from France in 1919, after fighting in the Marne and Argonne campaigns.

**A patriotic women's group,** one of many that helped raise spirits and funds for the war effort, parades down Broad Street, past the Masonic Temple. THE LIBRARY COMPANY OF PHILADELPHIA

**Gen. John "Black Jack" Pershing,** commander of U.S. forces in World War I, is welcomed to Philadelphia on Sept. 12, 1919, by Mayor Thomas B. Smith. THE LIBRARY COMPANY OF PHILADELPHIA

**The shadow of an approaching menace,** Hitler's Third Reich, falls over Philadelphia as the zeppelin Hindenburg visits the city on Aug. 8, 1936. While the touring ship's mission was peaceful, the swastikas on its tail presaged another war to come. Nine months later, on May 6, 1937, the airship blew up over Lakehurst, N.J.

FREE LIBRARY OF PHILADELPHIA /
PRINT AND PICTURE COLLECTION /
AERO SERVICE

**The Draft Bowl,** used for drawing draft numbers in 1917, is removed from storage at Independence Hall and prepared to be taken to Washington in 1941 for use again. The United States in 1940 instituted the first peacetime draft in its history. Almost 246,000 Philadelphians registered. THE PHILADELPHIA INQUIRER

**By 1942 security had tightened,** and police were on the lookout for draft-dodgers. Here, police halt cars along Delaware Avenue to check draft cards and seek to prevent sabotage.

THE PHILADELPHIA INQUIRER

**Two days after Pearl Harbor,** troops return to their barracks at Fort Dix, N.J., from a training exercise, shouting, "On to Tokyo!"

THE PHILADELPHIA INQUIRER / JESSE HARTMAN

**Rationing was the government's way** of dealing with wartime shortages. The red and blue ration coupons, and various other stickers, were needed for items in short supply: gasoline, tires, shoes, cigarettes, meat, sugar, coffee, liquor. In administering the system, local rationing boards took into account a family's size, type of work, distance to the job, and health. But black markets flourished.

THE PHILADELPHIA INQUIRER / OTTO C. PRINZ

**In the early years of the war,** people took civil defense seriously, including being fitted for gas masks. Rebecca Reese gets her mask adjusted in October 1941 by a member of the Pennsylvania Military Training Corps. THE PHILADELPHIA INQUIRER

**"Rosie the Riveter"** and thousands like her moved into war work, replacing men who'd gone to fight. Less well known was the practice of using midgets — "little men" who could get into places where the average-sized person was unable to navigate. Helped by Harry Newman of Uniontown, Kathryn Holdeman rivets part of a wing in the aircraft factory at the Navy Yard in 1943. THE PHILADELPHIA INQUIRER

**Women defense workers in 1943** rivet the turret for the waist-gun compartment of a Navy bomber, as the rest of the plane takes shape.
The only airplane factory owned and operated by the U.S. Navy was at the Philadelphia Navy Yard, which had one of the largest aeronautical
research laboratories in America. The Navy's first flying boats were built here. THE PHILADELPHIA INQUIRER

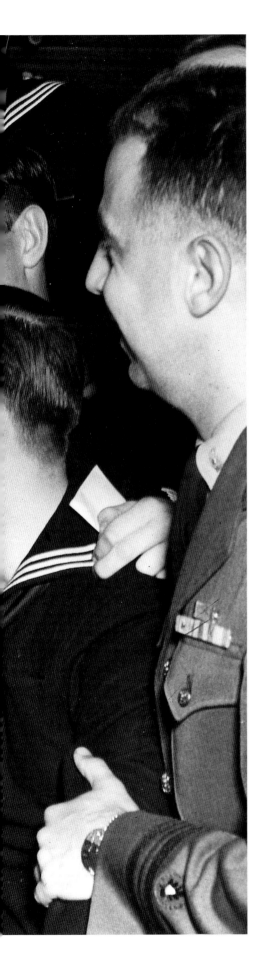

**Actress Gertrude Lawrence** is surrounded by servicemen in October 1942, after a performance at the Stage Door Canteen in the basement of the Academy of Music. Hospitality centers for on-leave servicemen and women, the canteens and United Service Organization (USO) centers were staffed by volunteers and witnessed many a budding romance.

THE PHILADELPHIA INQUIRER / HARRY RAYNORR

**Patients at the Navy Hospital** put on a show for their colleagues in March 1945. By this time, it took a lot to make wounded veterans laugh — but these guys succeeded.

THE PHILADELPHIA INQUIRER / HOWARD HAMBURGER

**As peace breaks out,** there's free beer for all at a spontaneous party in the 1100 block of Huntingdon Street in North Philadelphia. The moment Japan's surrender was announced on Aug. 14, 1945, Mayor Bernard Samuel ordered all the bars in town to close, but the celebratory thirst was not to be denied. THE PHILADELPHIA INQUIRER

**Lunch-hour dances** keep workers at the William Cramp and Sons shipyard fit and happy in June 1943. But under the strain of long hours and frozen wages, workers staged a one-day strike that fall.

INQUIRER ARCHIVES

**Victory is bittersweet for many.** John Morelli, a 23-year-old sergeant from Leavenworth, Kan., negotiates through the victory confetti at City Hall on Aug. 14, 1945. He was wounded and held prisoner in Germany for eight months.

THE PHILADELPHIA INQUIRER

**The Korean War** was the first for the U.S. Air Force. Col. Raymond M. Gehrig pins the Air Medal on Francis P. Burns Jr., 9, of Drexel Hill. The medal was awarded posthumously in 1952 to the boy's father, a pilot killed during the Korean War. The ceremony was at St. Joseph's College. THE PHILADELPHIA INQUIRER

**Lt. J. Stacey Baird** is one of "the amps," as those who lost limbs in the Vietnam War dubbed themselves. The year is 1971, a decade into America's involvement in that war, and Baird is practicing on his new leg at Valley Forge Army Hospital.

THE PHILADELPHIA INQUIRER

**Pain and pride mark the faces of Vietnam vets** at the unveiling of the Philadelphia Vietnam War Memorial, at Front and Spruce Streets near Penn's Landing, on Oct. 26, 1987. THE PHILADELPHIA INQUIRER / MYRNA LUDWIG

# Hometown Celebrities

THE CENTURY PROVED LUCKY. When it came to celebrities, Philadelphia was dealt a royal flush: a glorious princess, a fresh prince, a king of comedy, Four Aces, a series of sublime jokers. All began their celebrated lives in the city's environs.

Grace Kelly, born to an East Falls dynasty, was that uncommon commoner: She looked more regal than royalty itself, developing a cool, ethereal look that never faded from style. Then Kelly pulled off the hat trick, captivating Hollywood, the country, and a prince.

With a Cheshire-cat grin, Wynnefield's Will Smith became a crown prince of entertainment, conquering music, TV, and movies. He was following a path Bill Cosby had paved before him. Cosby, Temple University's proudest alumnus, became an entertainment conglomerate.

**Rocky triumphant,** atop the Art Museum steps. THE PHILADELPHIA INQUIRER / VICKI VALERIO

Philadelphia, a haven of firsts, could have been Hollywood. Before incandescent stars fell out of the city and winged their way west, Siegmund Lubin – an ophthalmologist by trade – created the world's first movie studio in Philadelphia, producing 2,500 silent movies during the century's early

**Grace Kelly of East Falls** gave up her Hollywood crown to become Princess Grace of Monaco, marrying Prince Rainier in Monte Carlo on April 19, 1956. INQUIRER ARCHIVES / UNITED PRESS INTERNATIONAL

years. Lubin shot westerns in Drexel Hill. He blew up city warehouses for the sake of art. He was the master of the disaster flick, filming train crashes, mining cave-ins, earthquakes. Lubinville, the lot at 20th and Indiana, played host to John Barrymore (of the city's royal stage family), Mary Pickford and Cecil B. DeMille.

The nation's singing sweetheart, Jeanette MacDonald (who made eight movies with Nelson Eddy), came from Philadelphia. So did wide-eyed Janet Gaynor, who went on to capture the first Academy Award in 1928.

W.C. Fields, the original grouch, the dipsomaniacal disparager of children and canines, grew up as William Claude Dukenfield in poverty around the city. He worked at Strawbridge & Clothier before taking to the vaudeville circuit. "Last week I went to Philadelphia, but it was closed," he once said. But contrary to popular wisdom, "All things considered, I'd rather be in Philadelphia" is not carved on his tombstone.

**Will Smith** of Wynnefield went from rap to TV to smash films.

INQUIRER ARCHIVES / ASSOCIATED PRESS

Larry Fine, the curliest of the knuckleheaded Three Stooges, was first Louis Feinberg of Third and South. He was a boxer and violin player before serving four decades of hard comic time.

Joyous noise poured out of the city's street corners and school gyms to create indelible sound. South Philadelphia kids like Frankie Avalon and Fabian Forte went on to become teen sensations. Al Alberts attended South Philadelphia High and Temple before creating the Four Aces.

Musicians are, by nature, an itinerant sort, and none more so than jazz performers. But many legends found root in the city. John Coltrane, a towering genius of jazz, moved to South Philadelphia at 18 and later to Strawberry Mansion, to begin a stunning career. John "Dizzy" Gillespie, one of the century's great trumpet players, moved to Sixth and Pine at age 18. He played his first professional gig at the Green Gate Inn at 12th and Bainbridge. The inimitable tenor sax player Stan Getz was born in South Philadelphia. Bassist Stanley Clarke, Jimmy

Heath, Johnny Coles and Lee Morgan began here. Before fathering West Coast cool, Gerry Mulligan was roaming the halls of West Catholic High.

The sounds of Philadelphia grew louder south on Broad, the snapping fingers and seductive vocalizing emanating from South Philly corners. It was a town of crooners, Eddie Fisher and Al Martino. The teenage look of the 1950s and '60s, high hair and sharp suits, came straight out of Philadelphia. Bobby Rydell and James Darren, Avalon and Forte, these city kids melted the hearts of many an overheated teenage girl, cranking out hit 45s and movies that were testaments to summer love.

Dick Clark was there to send it out to the nation. From 1957 to 1964, the national dance show *American Bandstand* was headquartered at WFIL studios at 46th and Market. The never-subtle Phil Spector dubbed the town "the most insane, the most dynamite, the most beautiful city in the history of rock and roll and the world." And local hoofers became pop phenomenons, dance teachers to an eager nation, shaking the afternoon away to incessant hits like Chubby Checker's "The Twist."

Kenneth Gamble and Leon Huff created the lush, soulful hits of the '70s, branding their "Sound of Philadelphia" with Philadelphia International Records. Among their greatest homegrown recordings were Billy Paul's "Me and Mrs. Jones," the O'Jays' "Love Train," and Harold Melvin and the Blue Notes' plaintive "If You Don't Know Me by Now."

Sylvester Stallone, born in New York and raised in Maryland, lived in the area for only a few years in high school and while shooting a quintet of pugilist pictures. But to the nation, Philadelphia may be most strongly identified on film with *Rocky* (1976), encouraging a legion of tourists to tirelessly bound up the Art Museum steps and pose at the top, fists held straight and high, in triumph over the city. ∎

**Siegmund Lubin** (inset) founded the world's first movie studio in the city, making 2,500 films between 1896 and 1923.

FREE LIBRARY OF PHILADELPHIA / THEATER COLLECTION

**William Claude Dukenfield** rose from ungenteel poverty in the city to become W.C. Fields, a unique comic voice. He worked at Strawbridge & Clothier before joining the Ziegfeld Follies in 1915. INQUIRER ARCHIVES / UNITED PRESS INTERNATIONAL

**Nelson Eddy and Jeanette MacDonald,** America's singing sweethearts, got their start here. She was born and educated in West Philly, and he made his 1922 singing debut at the Academy of Music. They made eight highly successful movies together. INQUIRER ARCHIVES / MGM

**A gentle comic and clown, Ed Wynn,** who attended Central High, won fame in the early 1930s. He triumphed on Broadway, then radio, movies, and early TV before turning to dramatic roles. INQUIRER ARCHIVES / NBC

**On the bottom, Louis Feinberg** of Third and South became Larry Fine, one of the Three Stooges, in 1925. He is pictured with Moe Howard (top) and Curly Joe DeRita, also born here, who joined the act in 1958. The Stooges disbanded in 1970. INQUIRER ARCHIVES

**Fred Waring and the Pennsylvanians,** a dance band, toured for six decades, beginning in the 1920s. The group played with such entertainment giants as Frank Sinatra. Waring is famous on another front: The blender in which he invested bears his name. INQUIRER ARCHIVES / WILLIAM MORRIS AGENCY

**Representative of the many community orchestras** at the turn of the century was Philadelphia's Treble Clef String Orchestra, shown here in 1910.

THE LIBRARY COMPANY OF PHILADELPHIA

**Paul Whiteman was the "King of Jazz"** in the 1920s and '30s, launching the Big Band era. He later hosted *TV Teen Club* Saturday nights on WFIL, which was televised nationally in the 1950s.

**Irrepressible showstoppers Pearl Bailey (left) and Ethel Waters** both hailed from these parts. Bailey, a dancer, singer, and talk show host, appeared in the movie *Carmen Jones* and toured widely in *Hello, Dolly!* Waters, born in Chester, won wide acclaim as a dancer, singer, and dramatic actress, most notably on stage in *A Member of the Wedding* and in her Academy Award-nominated performance for the movie *Pinky*.

INQUIRER ARCHIVES / NBC TELEVISION

**Ethel Waters in 1971.**

INQUIRER ARCHIVES / UNITED PRESS INTERNATIONAL

**The legendary John Coltrane** was one of the giants of jazz. The saxophone player moved to South Philadelphia at 18 and later to Strawberry Mansion, where he lived for most of the 1950s. Coltrane died at age 40 in 1967. His house, at 1511 North 33rd Street, has been turned into a Coltrane memorial. INQUIRER ARCHIVES / BRAVO NETWORK

**Two Franks and a heap of pasta:** Frank Palumbo and Frank Sinatra feasting at Palumbo's famed South Philadelphia eatery circa 1950. INQUIRER ARCHIVES

**Eddie Fisher,** pictured here in 1953, broke the heart of many a Philly girl before marrying Debbie Reynolds, whom he left for Elizabeth Taylor. As a crooner, he is best known for his renditions of "Lady of Spain" and "Oh, Mein Papa."
BALCH INSTITUTE FOR ETHNIC STUDIES

**South Philadelphia singer Al Martino,** with his arm around a very young and then horn-playing Frankie Avalon, in an undated photo from the 1940s.
INQUIRER ARCHIVES

**The Four Aces,** one of many 1950s singing groups to get
their start in the city, featured Al Alberts, who went on to host
a long-running TV show for tots. They are (clockwise from left)
Dave Mahoney, Lou Silvestri, Sod Vaccaro, and Alberts.

INQUIRER ARCHIVES / DECCA RECORDS

**The Dixie Hummingbirds,** one of the country's premier gospel ensembles,
have been making music since 1928. In the '60s, they brought the
audience to its feet at the Newport Folk Festival. They were at a low
point in 1973 when Paul Simon picked them to sing "Loves Me Like
a Rock" on his second solo album. The 'Birds cut their own version
afterward, winning them a Grammy. INQUIRER ARCHIVES

**Rocking around the clock with Bill Haley and His Comets**
was all the rage in the 1950s. Haley signed with the
Philadelphia record label Essex in 1950 but did not
become a huge star until the song took off in 1955.
At his death in 1981, Haley had sold 60 million records.

INQUIRER ARCHIVES / DECCA RECORDS

**At Greenwich Recreation Center, Fourth and Shunk Streets,** actor and singer James Darren, then 22, meets his burgeoning legion of fans in 1958.

As teenagers in South Philadelphia, Frankie Avalon (left) and Bobby Rydell first teamed up as Rocco and the Saints. Avalon became prince of the beach in movies with Annette Funicello. INQUIRER ARCHIVES

**Bobby Rydell, born Robert Ridarelli,** grew up at 2400 South 11th Street. His hits include "Volare" and "Wildwood Days." He starred as a teen heartthrob in the 1963 movie *Bye Bye Birdie*. INQUIRER ARCHIVES / CAMEO RECORDS

**The eternal teenager Dick Clark launched** *American Bandstand* from WFIL's studios at 46th and Market. From 1957 to '64, Philadelphia teenagers taught the country how to dance, becoming celebrities in their own right. THE PHILADELPHIA INQUIRER / MICHAEL VIOLA

**Let's twist again, with Chubby Checker!** Checker's first and biggest hit, "The Twist," was in the Top 10 in 1960, and again in 1962.

INQUIRER ARCHIVES / COLUMBIA PICTURES

**Soft pretzel-hearted comic David Brenner** (left) appears on *The Mike Douglas Show*. From 1965 to 1978, Douglas, the nice guy of talk shows, hosted his national TV program from KYW studios. INQUIRER ARCHIVES / GROUP W PRODUCTIONS

Rehearsing with his South Philadelphia band, the Crystals, fabulous Fabian Forte became so popular with the girls that he no longer needed a last name. He is pictured here in 1959, at age 16.

INQUIRER ARCHIVES

Music producers Kenny Gamble (seated) and Leon Huff created some of the greatest soul hits of the 1970s with their "Sound of Philadelphia." Billy Paul, the O'Jays, and Harold Melvin and the Blue Notes all recorded with the power duo's Philadelphia International Records.

THE PHILADELPHIA INQUIRER / ROBERT L. MOONEY

**The pioneer of bebop, John Birks "Dizzy" Gillespie,** came to Philadelphia at the age of 18 and lived at Sixth and Pine. He made his professional musical debut at the Green Gate Inn and became one of the legends of American jazz. INQUIRER ARCHIVES / UNITED PRESS INTERNATIONAL

**Stan Getz was born in South Philadelphia** in 1927 and went on to become one of jazz's foremost tenor saxophonists, exploring South American rhythms. He is perhaps best known for "Girl from Ipanema," his 1964 collaboration with Brazilian singer Astrud Gilberto.

INQUIRER ARCHIVES

**Prior to founding West Coast cool, Gerry Mulligan** attended West Catholic High. An innovative baritone sax player, he formed his first quartet in 1952 with Chet Baker and later toured internationally with a 13-piece concert jazz band in the '60s. INQUIRER ARCHIVES / VERVE RECORDS

**Born in 1942 in Philadelphia, singer-songwriter Jim Croce** (with his wife, Ingrid) attended Villanova before launching a short but powerful musical career. Among his hits were "Bad, Bad Leroy Brown" and "Operator." He died in a 1973 plane crash.

THE PHILADELPHIA INQUIRER / ROBERT LATHAM

**Song stylist Teddy Pendergrass,** part of the lush Sound of Philadelphia, grew up in North Philadelphia before joining Harold Melvin and the Blue Notes in the 1970s as lead singer. He became a huge sex symbol and soul star. In March 1982, Pendergrass crashed his Rolls-Royce on Lincoln Drive, leaving him a quadriplegic, though he continues to perform.

THE PHILADELPHIA INQUIRER / AKIRA SUWA

**Gospel star Clara Ward** was lead singer of the Ward Singers, one of the most popular groups of the 1950s and '60s. She got her start performing at Ebenezer Baptist Church in North Philadelphia. Ward sang at the 1957 Newport Jazz Festival and the Village Vanguard. She died in 1973. INQUIRER ARCHIVES / JOE ALPER

**Grover Washington Jr., a jazz saxophonist,** long made his home in West Mount Airy. He was credited with inventing the sweet saxophone sound that is the backbone of smooth jazz. Here he's performing at a 1985 concert in Fairmount Park. Washington died in 1999; a Philadelphia middle school bears his name.

PHILADELPHIA DAILY NEWS / BOB LARAMIE

**Our star, Sally Starr,** was a staple of local children's entertainment on radio and television in the 1950s and '60s. She is in her cowgirl regalia during a promotional drive for WJMJ Radio in 1957. BALCH INSTITUTE FOR ETHNIC STUDIES LIBRARY / STANTON-HONORS AND AWARDS COLLECTION

**The cutup of the Rat Pack, Joey Bishop** returns to South Philadelphia in 1970 for a hot dog at Levis Old Original Restaurant. The standup comic was a regular on the Las Vegas Strip. His father had a bicycle store on Moyamensing Avenue.

INQUIRER ARCHIVES / MARK M. WEINGRAD

**Philadelphia was immortalized on film by Sylvester Stallone's Rocky,** the Italian Stallion, who practiced his punches in a meat locker. Here, he's strolling down Chestnut Street in 1978, while filming the second of his six *Rocky* movies.

THE PHILADELPHIA INQUIRER / MICHAEL VIOLA

**Daryl Hall (left) and John Oates teamed up at Temple** before producing a series of top pop hits in the 1970s and '80s, including "Maneater," "Kiss on My List," and "I Can't Go for That." The duo, known for a distinctive brand of "blue-eyed soul," recorded a local favorite called "Fall in Philadelphia." THE PHILADELPHIA INQUIRER / CHERIE KEMPER-STARNER

**Sun Ra, founder of his out-there Arkestra,** could have lived anywhere in the cosmos, but came to settle in Germantown.

THE PHILADELPHIA INQUIRER / RON TARVER

**R&B diva Patti LaBelle** whoops it up during a 1987 performance in Philadelphia, where she still lives. She made her mark in the 1960s with Patti LaBelle and the Bluebells, then went on to form the 1970s power trio LaBelle, best known for "Lady Marmalade." Then came a successful solo career. PHILADELPHIA DAILY NEWS / RICK BOWMER

**The latest smash group with Philadelphia roots is Boyz II Men,** the R&B quartet that got its start in 1985 at Philadelphia's High School for Creative and Performing Arts. The Boyz — (from left) Michael S. McCary, Nathan Morris, Wanya Morris, and Sean Stockman — gather at their plaque on the Philadelphia Music Walk of Fame on South Broad Street. Their first album, with Motown, was in 1991. They built their reputation on a clean, boy-next-door image, filming several of their videos here, including the hit "Motownphilly." THE PHILADELPHIA INQUIRER / DIRK SHADD

# The BIG Stories

IN ANY CITY, in any era, the events that dominate the headlines are heavy on disaster. And Philadelphia in the 20th century had more than its share.

Foremost in that roster of misery was a unique, self-inflicted debacle captured in a single word: MOVE. The events of May 13, 1985, turned Philadelphia into the city that bombed itself.

MOVE was a small back-to-nature cult that sprang up early in the 1970s. In 1978, a confrontation between it and Philadelphia police led to a shootout in which one officer was killed and a cult member was kicked and beaten in full view of news cameras. That set the stage for what was to come.

By 1985, MOVE had set up new headquarters at 6221 Osage Avenue and had turned it into an armed fortress. After negotiations failed, police surrounded the house. At dawn on May 13, Police Commissioner Gregore Sambor demanded surrender, proclaiming through a bullhorn, "Attention, MOVE. This is America."

A furious gun battle erupted, followed by long hours of silence. Then, at 5:27 p.m., a police helicopter dropped a satchel filled with explosives. Officials let the resulting fire burn. By the time they decided to put it out, it was too late.

**In 1978,** children were evacuated after a clash between police and MOVE, a back-to-nature cult.

THE PHILADELPHIA INQUIRER / WILLIAM F. STEINMETZ

**On the day after the 1985 bombing** of the MOVE house, authorities remove bodies. The fire that erupted after a bomb was dropped from a police helicopter gutted a city block and killed 11 people.

THE PHILADELPHIA INQUIRER / ED HILLE

The fire killed 11 residents of the MOVE house, five of them children, destroyed a block of 61 rowhouses — and forever marred the administration of W. Wilson Goode, the city's first black mayor.

"I watched everything I had worked for all my life go up in smoke," he would say later. "The deaths of those children, of those people, continue to haunt me."

There were times that Philadelphia was in the spotlight for more positive reasons, of course. Among them: July 4, 1976, the nation's 200th birthday. The celebration began at Valley Forge, where President Gerald R. Ford proclaimed the site of George Washington's winter encampment a national park. In the afternoon, thousands passed by the Liberty Bell, housed in a new, glass-enclosed pavilion. The day closed with a huge fireworks display.

Everything had gone just right. Three weeks later, out of nowhere, something went terribly wrong.

During the annual convention of the Pennsylvania American Legion, people started dropping dead. The toll reached 34, all but five of them delegates who'd gathered at the Bellevue Stratford, Philadelphia's grand old hotel. It took months to track down the killer, a previously unknown bacterium, and for scientists to give it a name, Legionnaires' disease.

Beyond these events, the litany of disasters is truly breathtaking.

On April 10, 1917, the Eddystone ammunition plant along the Delaware River exploded, killing 139 workers, most of them young women. Since the United States had entered World War I just four days earlier, there were suspicions, never proven, of international sabotage.

In 1918, the great influenza epidemic, which killed at least 25 million worldwide, hit Philadelphia harder than anywhere else in America. The city's death toll reached 13,000. Scores of soldiers, wounded in the fighting in Europe, came home to Philadelphia to recover, only to die from the flu.

Five years later, on June 11, 1923, the vast train shed at Broad Street Station, which spanned an acre and a half from 15th to 17th Streets west of City Hall, burned to the ground. Remarkably, no one was killed.

**A Middletown, Pa., resident** wears a T-shirt expressing the town's sentiments.

INQUIRER ARCHIVES / UNITED PRESS INTERNATIONAL

In another railroad disaster, on Sept. 6, 1943, the Congressional Limited, speeding from Washington to New York, crashed in Kensington, killing 79. Mechanical problems were blamed.

In late March 1979, a cooling system malfunction at a nuclear power plant at Three Mile Island, near Harrisburg, produced the threat of a nuclear meltdown and ten days of panic in eastern Pennsylvania.

Then there was the towering inferno: a fire that broke out Feb. 23, 1991, on the 22nd floor of One Meridian Plaza, a 38-story office tower across from City Hall. It burned for 19 hours, killing three firefighters and leaving the building an eyesore on the skyline for years.

Sometimes, the big story was the important people who came to town. In 1948, both major parties staged their nominating conventions in Philadelphia, the Democrats selecting President Harry S Truman, the Republicans picking New York Gov. Thomas E. Dewey. The city previously had hosted the Democrats and Franklin Roosevelt in 1936, the Republicans and Wendell Willkie in 1940 and the GOP convention that chose William McKinley in 1900. In 1976, challenger Jimmy Carter and President Ford debated at the Walnut Street Theatre — until a power outage caused them to stand in silence for 28 minutes. In 1997, President Bill Clinton, with former Presidents Carter, Ford and George Bush, hosted a three-day summit on volunteerism.

Pope John Paul II spent a memorable 21 hours in the city in October 1979, a stay highlighted by a magnificent open-air Mass at Logan Circle. Britain's Queen Elizabeth II came to visit, and the Beatles did, too.

And what was perhaps the most significant event of the Philadelphia century went largely unnoticed. On Feb. 14, 1946, engineers at the University of Pennsylvania unveiled the first modern computer, the Electronic Numerical Integrator and Calculator, ENIAC for short. Although an *Inquirer* reporter wrote that it heralded "a new epoch of human thought," the story made no immediate waves. It ran on page 9, tucked between two fashion ads. ■

Where Is the War Leading Us?
'Phone or Write—The Inquirer Does the Rest

Who Knows
'Phone or Write—The Inquirer Does

# The Philadelphia Inquirer

VOL. 176, NO. 101      TODAY'S WEATHER—Fair      PHILADELPHIA, WEDNESDAY MORNING, APRIL 11, 1917      TWO CENT

# 122 KILLED, 150 INJURED, MAJORITY WOMEN, BY EXPLOSION LAID TO PLOTTERS IN PLANT OF EDDYSTONE AMMUNITION CORPORATION

THE PANORAMIC VIEW OF THE DESTROYED BUILDINGS GIVES AN EXCELLENT IDEA OF THE HAVOC WROUGHT BY THE EXPLOSION AT THE EDDYSTONE AMMUNITION PLANT. "OLD F" AND "NEW F" CAN EASILY BE DISTINGUISHED, FORMER BEING LOCATED TO THE RIGHT. IT WAS HERE THAT SO MANY WORKERS WERE KILLED. THE EXPLOSION LAID THE STRUCTURES WASTE. A WATCHBOX IS LOCATED IN THE FOREGROUND.

## ELEVEN THOUSAND GERMANS CAPTURED BY BRITISH DRIVE

Push Wedge Five Miles Deeper in Teuton Lines, Seizing 160 Large and 163 Small Guns

BY ARTHUR S. DRAPER

LONDON, April 10.—General Haig's "big push" has swept on today almost from La Basse to St. Quentin and driven a wedge into the very vitals of the German front five miles beyond Monday morning's line at Arras.

The number of German prisoners has almost doubled since yesterday. It now exceeds 11,000, including 235 officers, and the total promises to reach 16,000 before midnight.

The victors have counted over 160 guns, among them a number of Krupp monsters of eight-inch calibre, 60 trench mortars and 163 machine guns.

Despite heavy snowstorms and tenacious resistance by the Germans, the British infantry, clad in heavy sheepskins, is advancing so fast that the line must be revised from hour to hour.

The new front now runs almost from the outskirts of La Basse beyond Loos, just this side of Lens, east of the Vimy ridge, now firmly held by the Canadians along its entire range.

Continued on 4th Page, 5th Col.

### LOST AND FOUND

### German Loss Heavy in Men and Guns

In the two days of the British drive the Germans lost 11,000 prisoners, including 235 officers.

Monster Krupp guns to the number of more than 100, together with 60 mortars and 163 machine guns, fell to the English.

## ARGENTINE FOLLOWS BRAZIL IN BREAK WITH THE KAISER

Sensation When News Is Received—May Mobilize at Once

BUENOS AIRES, Argentina, April 10.—The government issued a declaration this evening announcing that it supported the position of the United States in reference to Germany.

The declaration was made known to the public through bulletins posted throughout the city and caused a great sensation. Some of the newspapers say that high officers of the army assert that the military mobilization of Argentina will follow that of Brazil.

RIO JANEIRO, April 10.—At a Cabinet Council today it was decided that Brazil should sever her relations with Germany.

The official action regarding the sinking of the Brazilian steamship Parana, which the Brazilian steamship Parana, caused the government has been awaiting before taking definite action toward Germany, is believed to have been received today from the location in the press statement at Berlin.

[handwritten letter:]
To the Inquirer
Regarding the terrible Catastrophe which happened at the Eddystone Ammunition Corporation Plant this morning. We are unable to account for it in any way other than the act of some maliciously inclined person or persons.
Yours truly
S. M. Vauclain

SAMUEL M. VAUCLAIN DECLARES PLANT WAS BLOWN UP

## MAYOR WILL DEMAND MILITIA; THREEFOLD EXPLOSION PROBE ON

Aroused by the explosion at Eddystone, Mayor Smith will ask at once to have State troops sent here to guard munition plants, steel works and machine shops capable of turning out the necessities of war. Federal, State and local investigations are being made to determine the causes of the disaster that ended more than 100 lives, resulted in the wounding of an equal number of men and women and wrecked the shrapnel loading building of the Eddystone Ammunition Corporation's plant yesterday.

Little doubt existed in the minds of those edited from the plottings of an individual or individuals.

The investigators learned many things that strengthened their belief that the tragedy resulted from a plot.

Half a dozen suspected workmen were taken into custody by the guards at the munition plant yesterday. All were released. No "official" arrests were made until night.

### Gabarine Heads U. S. Probe

Special Agent Frank L. Garbarino, chief of the Philadelphia office of the Bureau of Investigation of the United States Department of Justice, is at the head of the probe for the Federal authorities.

## SHRAPNEL VOLLEYS WITHER TRAPPED SURVIVORS OF FIRST BLAST; RIGID FEDERAL PROBE O

Bodies of Victims So Badly Mangled That Many Will Never Be Identified—Some Blown Into Delaware River—Father and Son, Latter an Employe, Arrested by Guardsmen

One hundred and twenty-two persons were killed and one hundred and fifty injured in a series of three explosions which destroyed one of the buildings of the Eddystone Ammunition Corporation, Eddystone, Pa., yesterday morning.

The majority of the dead and injured are women and girls. Ten of the injured will die. Many bodies are so terribly mangled that identification is impossible. Fragments of bodies, arms, legs and trunks were found within the radius of a square of the plant. Several bodies are believed to be in the Delaware.

All of the victims lived in Philadelphia and Chester and in the district between the two cities. A complete list of the victims will not be available until the company checks up its list of employes.

### BELIEVES EXPLOSIONS PLANNED

The explosions, according to Samuel M. Vauclain, president of the corporation, were planned and executed by maliciously inclined person or persons.

Basil Grenfal, a Russian inspector, who was in the building when the explosions occurred declared that a bomb had been used.

This is also the belief of secret service men who are working on the case, though Federal rules prohibit them from expressing an opinion.

At Chester last night two suspects, father and son, the latter an employe in the plant, were arrested. They are being held pending an investigation.

### FEDERAL AGENTS ACTIVE

Frank L. Garbarino, in charge of the local bureau of the Department of Justice, is directing the investigation for the government. Independent investigations are being made by the State of Pennsylvania, Delaware County, the Philadelphia police and the officials of the corporation.

All develop evidence that the mind that directed the bomb outrages and incendiary fires in America during the early part of the European war is again active.

It is regarded as possible that Philadelphia has been selected as the scene for the beginning of new reign of terrorism, now that America has thrown her lot with the

principals are expected without delay. Government officials declare that the most drastic measures against tile aliens will be taken.

The arrests of the two suspects were made shortly 10 o'clock and only after the officials had made a and rigid investigation. Late last night an officer National Guard declared that the investigators look the arrests as one of the most important developm the day. Papers found on one of the men were de "incriminating and very important!"

The younger man gave his name as Samuel Ca years old, of 656 South Forty-third street. He Chester Hospital under guard.

The older man, it was declared, was well with money. Neither, it is said, was a citizen United States. The older man was taken away by men in an automobile.

### CITY'S GREATEST DEATH TOLL

The toll of death yesterday was the greatest
Continued on 2d Page, 1st Col.

### Identified Dead

The identified dead at 10 o'clock last night were:
BERTHA R. FINNEGAN, 17 North Eighth street, Chester.
BERTHA ORDWAY, 704 ninth street, Chester.
ANNIE N. MEGARY,
SAMUEL KOWLESKI, 700 East Eighth street, Chester.
HATTIE GATES, 1000 Howard street, Eddystone, Pa.
MIKE MAGONE, 2005 Ford street, Chester.
ANNA STERN MALE, 342 McIntire street, Chester.
DOROTHY MAGUIRE, Bolton, Pa.
ANTHONY PARSONS, 4910 Woodland avenue, Philadelphia.
LEO PETTINGER, 1826 South First South street, Phila.
BEATRICE GLATHIEN, 613 South Orange street, Media, Pa.
ANNA SIPAR, 2002 Laycock avenue, Philadelphia.
MYRTLE FERRIGAN, Fifth street, Chester.
Continued on 2d Page, 7th Col.

### THE WEATHER

Forecast from Washington: For Eastern Pennsylvania, New Jersey, Delaware, Maryland and Western Pennsylvania, fair and warmer Wednesday, Thursday

### Perry's have in a Rising N

We don't mean we alone have escape tific rise in woolens materials, but we in those cases costs have been alway we have assumed the of the burden, protect our own expense, but ing institution protecttrons in a period of

There are no clothdelphia today which a affected by the advanvance in costs.

And there is no delphia which can show a wealth of variety Perry's can right now!

We're still retail service and satisfy the old figure!

SUITS

Single-Breasted
Double-Breasted

**The train shed of the Broad Street Station,** near City Hall, was destroyed by fire on June 11, 1923. The train tracks, which went west from the station, ran atop an elevated wall, which divided the city and came to be called the "Chinese wall." THE PHILADELPHIA INQUIRER

**The Congressional Limited,** carrying 541 passengers from Washington to New York, derailed in Kensington on Sept. 6, 1943. Seventy-nine people died, making it one of the nation's worst train disasters.

INQUIRER ARCHIVES / ACME NEWSPICTURES

**During the measles outbreak of 1941,** Gerald and Leon Masino were two of thousands of youngsters who were infected and quarantined.

TEMPLE URBAN ARCHIVES

**The great influenza epidemic of 1918,** a worldwide killer, devastated Philadelphia. In the course of two months, 13,000 residents died, many more Philadelphians than were killed in World War I.

TEMPLE URBAN ARCHIVES

All persons not occupants of this house are notified of the presence of

# MEASLES

within, and are warned not to enter it until this notice is removed. The person sick with this disease must not leave the house as long as this notice remains here.

By order of
### THE BOARD OF HEALTH

The Act of Assembly approved June 28, 1923, provides that any person or persons convicted of removing, defacing, covering up or destroying this placard shall be subject to a *fine* of not more than $100, or by *imprisonment* of not more than 30 days, or both.

**For protection against the flu,** people who had to deal with the public — police in particular — wore masks. Here, a police officer takes a man, wrapped in a blanket, into a hospital.

TEMPLE URBAN ARCHIVES

**The Depression** hit Philadelphia hard, beginning in 1930. Some homeless people lived in caves below the Art Museum along the Schuylkill, where they did their wash.
TEMPLE URBAN ARCHIVES

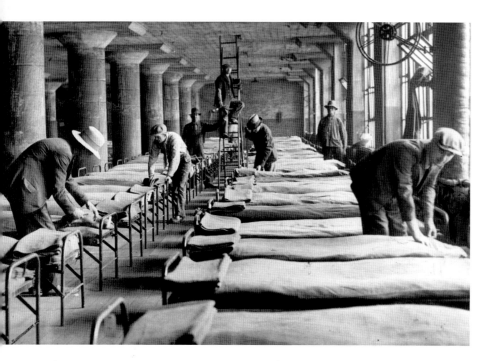

**Some homeless men found refuge** in a shelter set up at the former Baldwin Locomotive Works, 18th and Hamilton Streets. THE PHILADELPHIA INQUIRER

**As late as 1938,** thousands of Philadelphians were still lining up for unemployment checks. The Depression ended when war production geared up in the early 1940s.

THE PHILADELPHIA INQUIRER

**Strikes occurred throughout the century**, as Philadelphia became a strong labor town. In 1910, police on horseback pursued transit workers protesting the firing of 175 of their colleagues.

FREE LIBRARY OF PHILADELPHIA / PRINT AND PICTURE COLLECTION

**In 1944, Army troops** were sent in by President Roosevelt after white transit workers walked off the job in protest over the hiring of black motormen.

THE PHILADELPHIA INQUIRER

**Once World War II was over**, workers pressed for pay increases to match the inflation unleashed when wartime price controls came off. The result was an unprecedented number of strikes in 1945 and '46. An electrical workers' strike against a General Electric plant at 69th Street and Elmwood Avenue in February 1946 turned violent when police charged picketers, many of them veterans, and seized their flag. Union leader Harry Block lashed out at the "Gestapo tactics" and 8,000 to 10,000 G.E. strikers and sympathizers marched on City Hall.

**Seven national political conventions** have been held in the city since 1900, when the Republicans nominated William McKinley. In 1936, the Democrats nominated Franklin Delano Roosevelt (above) for a second term, and they chose Harry S Truman (right) in 1948. Also in 1948 the GOP picked Thomas E. Dewey here and the Progressives chose Henry Wallace. In 2000, Republicans nominated George W. Bush.

THE PHILADELPHIA INQUIRER

**Wendell Willkie was the nominee** when Republicans gathered in Philadelphia in 1940.

THE PHILADELPHIA INQUIRER / FRANK ROSS

**In 1975, a fire aboard the Liberian oil tanker Corinthos** in the Delaware off Marcus Hook killed 26 crew members.

THE PHILADELPHIA INQUIRER / CHARLES W. JAMES

**A Philadelphia version of** *Towering Inferno* occurred when the 38-story skyscraper at One Meridian Plaza, across from City Hall, caught fire on Feb. 23, 1991. The hulk scarred the skyline for almost a decade.

THE PHILADELPHIA INQUIRER / MICHAEL S. WIRTZ

**The body of Officer James Ramp** (left) and a wounded officer are removed by police while the siege continues. THE PHILADELPHIA INQUIRER / WILLIAM F. STEINMETZ

**Delbert Africa** raises his arms in surrender. THE PHILADELPHIA INQUIRER / JAMES G. DOMKE

**In the first confrontation between police and MOVE,** on Aug. 8, 1978, Officer James Ramp was shot and killed. His body and that of a wounded officer were removed (above left). As MOVE member Delbert Africa surrendered, he was kicked and beaten by police officers.

THE PHILADELPHIA INQUIRER / JAMES G. DOMKE

**The second MOVE confrontation,** on May 13, 1985, began when neighbors complained that MOVE members had turned their home in Cobbs Creek into a fortress. After a 12-hour standoff, police dropped a bomb from a helicopter. The public watched it live on television.

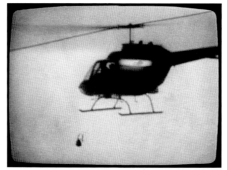

NBC 10/WCAU

THE PHILADELPHIA INQUIRER / GERALD S. WILLIAMS

**Two years after the siege,** Ramona Africa filed a civil suit against the city in federal court. After a 1996 trial, she was awarded $500,000.

THE PHILADELPHIA INQUIRER / TOM GRALISH

**The aftermath of MOVE II:** 61 houses burned, 11 people dead, and a city's reputation in shreds.

**The only MOVE survivors**
were Ramona Africa
(opposite page) and
13-year-old Birdie Africa.

**They called it "The Blizzard of '96"** — the biggest snowstorm in Philadelphia history. In less than three days, by Jan. 8 it had dumped 30.7 inches of snow, leaving the region looking like the 700 block of Annin Street in South Philadelphia. Lena Ruiz and her mother, Sissy Ruiz, try to dig out. THE PHILADELPHIA INQUIRER / MICHAEL S. WIRTZ

**Debris rained down on a playground** in Merion on April 4, 1991, after a small plane carrying U.S. Sen. John Heinz collided with a helicopter. Seven people died, including the senator and two children on the ground.

THE PHILADELPHIA INQUIRER / REBECCA BARGER

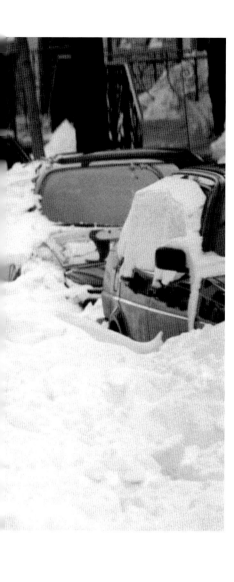

**A Legionnaires' disease survivor,** Albert Salmon, has his lungs tested in 1978, two years after the disease swept the American Legion's state convention at the Bellevue Stratford.

THE PHILADELPHIA INQUIRER / MICHAEL VIOLA

**Driving was disrupted for millions** of people in the 1970s by two major gasoline shortages caused by cutbacks in Arab oil production. At a protest in Levittown in 1979, demonstrators set a car afire. INQUIRER ARCHIVES / ASSOCIATED PRESS

**The city endured a series of strikes** by municipal workers in the 1970s and '80s. In the strike of 1986, uncollected trash piled up in the streets for 20 hot summer days. Here, sanitation workers block the entrance to an incinerator in Roxborough to protest a back-to-work court order.
THE PHILADELPHIA INQUIRER / MICHAEL VIOLA

**During the 1974 shortage,** some service stations, like this one in Morrisville, Pa., reserved their supplies for regular customers.
THE PHILADELPHIA INQUIRER / MICHAEL VIOLA

**Periodic storms battered the region.**
In 1962, a winter storm swept over
Harvey Cedars, N.J., on Long Beach Island.

INQUIRER ARCHIVES / U.S. ARMY CORPS OF ENGINEERS

**In 1972, Tropical Storm Agnes** flooded much of
Pennsylvania, making High Street in Pottstown
accessible only by boat.

THE PHILADELPHIA INQUIRER / ALEXANDER McCAUGHEY

**On his arrival in Philadelphia on Oct. 3, 1979**, Pope John Paul II was greeted by Mayor Frank L. Rizzo and Cardinal John Krol.

THE PHILADELPHIA INQUIRER / MICHAEL VIOLA

**Pope John Paul II celebrated Mass** at Logan Circle
before a crowd estimated at one million.
Here, the Pope's procession (lower right)
moves up the Parkway toward the altar.

THE PHILADELPHIA INQUIRER / ROBERT L. MOONEY

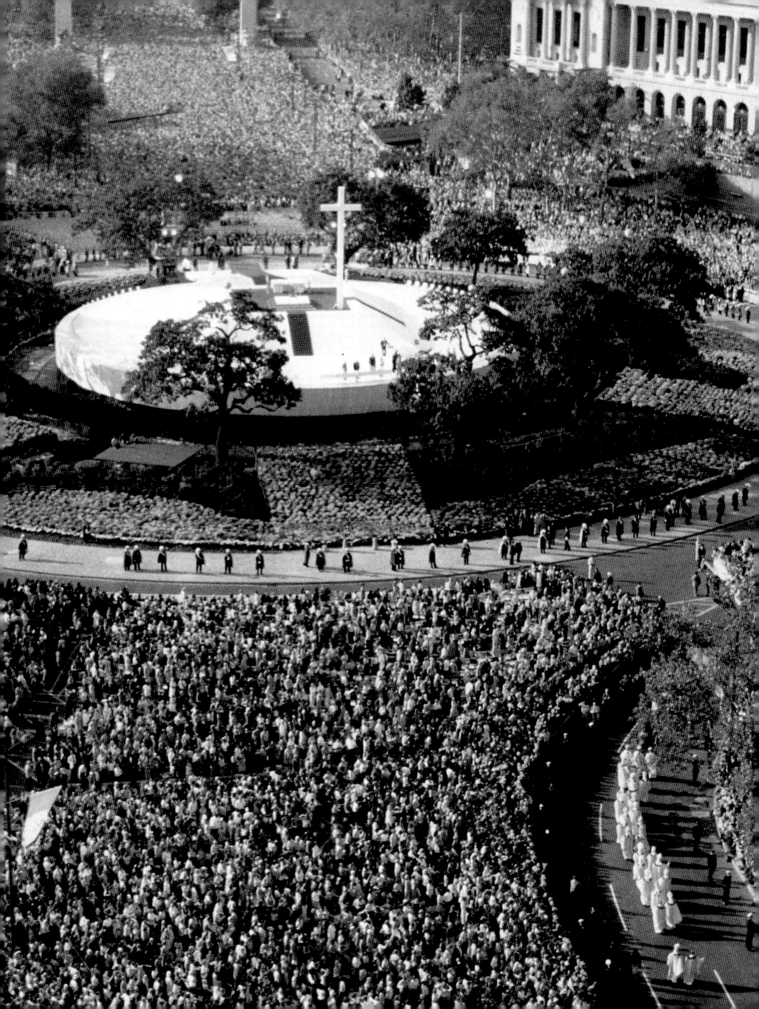

**It was the first accidental release of radiation** at a commercial nuclear power plant in America, and it panicked much of eastern Pennsylvania. The incident at Three Mile Island began on March 28, 1979. It was 10 days before officials gave the all-clear.

INQUIRER ARCHIVES / UNITED PRESS INTERNATIONAL

ALL VEHICLES STOP

ALL VISITORS COMMERCIAL VEHICLES

**Tom Fox of the Department of Energy** takes water samples from the Susquehanna River. INQUIRER ARCHIVES / UNITED PRESS INTERNATIONAL

**Outdoor extravaganzas** were a Philadelphia hallmark in the 1980s. The 1985 Live Aid concert, twinned with another in London, drew 100,000 to John F. Kennedy Stadium in South Philadelphia. The money raised went to feed the starving in sub-Saharan Africa. PHILADELPHIA DAILY NEWS / G. LOIE GROSSMANN

**Dazzling the audience,** Tina Turner and Mick Jagger perform a provocative duet. Other big-name acts included Bob Dylan, Joan Baez, Lionel Richie, Teddy Pendergrass, Dionne Warwick, and Crosby, Stills and Nash.

**The Live Aid stage** at JFK Stadium.

The Sesquicentennial Exposition of 1926, celebrating the nation's 150th birthday, was a disaster. It opened late, with roads unpaved, exhibits unfinished, and pavilions not done. Rain fell on 107 of the 184 days of the fair. The project did pave the way for the development of the southern end of the city. And a stadium built for "Sesqui," where 120,000 fans watched Gene Tunney beat Jack Dempsey, was the forerunner of the South Philadelphia sports complex. THE PHILADELPHIA INQUIRER

**A huge, lighted replica of the Liberty Bell** hung at the entrance to the Sesquicentennial Exposition grounds near League Island Park.

THE PHILADELPHIA INQUIRER

**Honoring 1776** and two hundred years of America, Philadelphia celebrated the Bicentennial in a big way. A day of speeches, parades, picnics, and concerts culminated with a massive fireworks display over the Benjamin Franklin Parkway.

THE PHILADELPHIA INQUIRER / RICHARD M. TITLEY

THESE
SEGREGATE
WALLS MUST
COME DOWN
AS THE
WALLS OF
JERICHO

# Social Movements

THREE GREAT SOCIAL REFORM MOVEMENTS transformed Philadelphia, and America, in the 20th century: the drive to enfranchise women, the black struggle for civil rights, and the youth culture of the 1960s that spearheaded protests against the Vietnam War. They shared one ideal — a commitment to inclusion in the nation's civic life — and practiced similar strategies.

The women's suffrage movement — featuring marching, chanting women in hobble skirts and hats — presented the most striking break with the past. The suffragettes' bold image stands in vivid contrast to the "genteel ideal" portrayed in the *Ladies' Home Journal*, an image of delicacy that held sway, despite the fact that by 1900 women made up 26 percent of the city's workforce, mostly in the textile industries.

**1972 peace rally,** Penn campus.

PHILADELPHIA DAILY NEWS /
JOSEPH J. McGUINN

Women of the middle and upper classes made strides — but obliquely, as they had for generations, working around or through husbands and brothers. Consider: Quaker Lydia Morris, founder of the Morris Arboretum, is often overshadowed by her brother John, although it was she who donated their Chestnut Hill estate to the public.

Even as privileged women supported settlement houses, training schools and women's colleges, some joined the struggle for women's suffrage. Notable among them was Lucretia Blankenburg, who led more than 100 women in a

**For nine months, the NAACP,** led by Cecil B. Moore (in tie), staged protests outside Girard College, a segregated boys' school. Ultimately, they prevailed. In 1968, Girard was integrated, by order of the U.S. Supreme Court. THE PHILADELPHIA INQUIRER / EDWARD J. FREEMAN

bold (for 1910) march down Broad Street.

World War I turned the tide. Leaders decided to hold off on protesting until after the hostilities. It was a shrewd decision, because the mobilization of women in the armed forces and in war industries helped boost their argument that women had earned the right to vote. The victory came in August 1920, with ratification of the 19th Amendment.

Women activists expanded their focus after World War II to fight nuclear testing and racial discrimination. History helps explain their activism: Philadelphia's Quakers were among the first to oppose slavery.

By 1899, blacks made up about five percent of the population. Many were descendants of free-born black Philadelphians, and thus constituted an insular, educated aristocracy. While many blacks agitated for fair treatment, few of these "OPs," or Old Philadelphians, did; they let their accomplishments speak for them.

The Wright family combined achievement with activism. Patriarch Major Richard R. Wright Sr. founded Philadelphia's first black-owned commercial bank, the Citizens and Southern Bank, in 1920. His son, Bishop Richard R. Wright Jr., documented 1,000 black businesses in his 1911 doctoral thesis, "The Negro in Pennsylvania." He helped run the bank and was a founder of the local NAACP in 1912. His daughter, Ruth Wright Hayre, racked up a long list of "firsts," including the first female president of the Board of Education.

Most OPs were taken aback by the great migration of black families, mostly uneducated farm workers, that began in the mid-1890s and ran through World War I. Like the waves of immigrants, these newcomers had to move into the poorest neighborhoods. Racial tensions rose as unskilled workers competed for jobs. In July 1918, riots broke out after a black woman moved into a white part of South Philly; four died in the four-day conflict.

Despite such chilling events, blacks made progress. In 1938, Crystal Bird Fauset of West Philadelphia became the first black woman in America elected to a state legislature. Eleanor Roosevelt regularly consulted with Fauset, a member of FDR's "black cabinet" of unofficial advisers.

In 1944 came another first: When white transit workers

**Icons of the '60s counterculture:**
Ira Einhorn and Abbie Hoffman.
THE PHILADELPHIA INQUIRER / ANTHONY RICCARDI

walked off the job to protest the upgrading of blacks to motormen and conductors, President Roosevelt sent troops on Aug. 5. Strikers were told they would lose their draft deferments if they did not return. The next day, the streetcars were running, blacks and whites working together. It marked the first time the federal government sent troops to protect the rights of black Americans.

As black veterans of World War II came home, the movement to end legal segregation picked up steam. The local NAACP took on new fervor when brash attorney Cecil B. Moore was elected president in 1962. He took the organization public in a big way, with street demonstrations, mass marches, and lawsuits.

In August 1964, simmering resentments in North Central Philadelphia exploded in a riot along Columbia Avenue; 339 people were hurt, two died, and much property was destroyed.

The NAACP persisted in protests, as the struggle became one for economic as well as civil justice. Its membership rose to 60,000 by 1967, largest in the nation. Blacks picketed the post office, bus terminals, department stores, drugstores. The campaigns won concessions on hiring and promotions.

The century's third significant movement brought together aging peaceniks and youthful hippies. Philadelphia has long been home to the American peace movement. In the 20th century, it hosted the Women's International League for Peace and Freedom and Women Strike for Peace. Now, activists protested the Vietnam War.

The late 1960s and early '70s were glory days for Philadelphia Resistance, a flamboyant peace group that held rallies, sit-ins and die-ins, and for Catholic activists like the Berrigan brothers, Philip and Daniel, a Jesuit priest. They and six others, known as the Plowshares Eight, were convicted in 1981 of splattering blood and smashing nose cones at a General Electric plant in King of Prussia.

As the 20th century wound down, so did mass protests. But their effects continue to ripple. ■

. . . . . . . . . . . . . . . . . . . . . . . . . . . . . . . . . . . . . . . . . . .

**Racism was not just a Southern phenomenon.** The Martha Washington Kamp No. 1 American Krusaders paraded in Frankford July 4, 1927.

THE TEMPLE URBAN ARCHIVES

**Suffragettes boldly take to the streets** in 1910. This demonstration, on Broad Street, took place 10 years before ratification of the 19th Amendment, granting women the right to vote.

TEMPLE URBAN ARCHIVES

**Lucretia Blankenburg,** photographed in 1914, was a civic and women's-rights leader and wife of the city's first reform mayor, Rudolph Blankenburg. INQUIRER ARCHIVES

**Many women, including Alice Stokes Paul** (center), realized that winning the vote would not ensure full legal equality. As early as 1910 the Quaker from Mount Laurel, N.J., began pushing an Equal Rights Amendment. In 1920 Alice Paul sews a star on the flag, symbolizing another state ratifying the Women's Suffrage Amendment. INQUIRER ARCHIVES / SWARTHMORE COLLEGE

**The Wright family** — Richard R. and his son, Bishop Richard R. Jr. — were among the leaders easing the migrants' way into the economic and civic life of the city.

WRIGHT FAMILY COLLECTION

**In 1922, Marcus Garvey's** Universal Negro Improvement Association was bent on helping blacks acquire training, jobs, housing, and self-determination. The Philadelphia Division was one of the nation's largest. PHILADELPHIA DAILY NEWS

**As Negroes migrated from the South,** long-established black Philadelphians set up self-help groups. Philadelphia, because of its Quaker and anti-slavery heritage, was considered hospitable to African Americans and their aspirations.

LIBRARY OF CONGRESS

**Kids in North Philadelphia** launch a neighborhood cleanup in the 1930s.

**Crystal Bird Fauset,** part of President Roosevelt's "black Cabinet," joins Eleanor Roosevelt at a 1942 rally in Washington. INQUIRER ARCHIVES / ASSOCIATED PRESS

**The messianic Father Divine** held sway over millions of followers, starting in the 1930s. He built black businesses and hotels, including the Divine Lorraine Hotel on North Broad Street, and brought his mission to Philadelphia in 1942.

THE PHILADELPHIA INQUIRER / DAN KELEHER

**At the 1948 Republican National Convention** in Philadelphia, demonstrators make their point.

INQUIRER ARCHIVES / ASSOCIATED PRESS

**Philadelphia neighborhoods** continued to be segregated well into the 1970s, and their schools were, too. This demonstration was in 1963.

THE PHILADELPHIA INQUIRER / ALBERT WAGNER

**One of the civil rights movement's great achievements** came in the fight to integrate Girard College, an all-white boys' school. For years, blacks had filed unsuccessful court challenges. Then the NAACP took the fight outdoors, with daily demonstrations. In September 1968, the school was opened to children of all races. The first African-American students to enter Founders Hall were Theodore L. Hicks, 9; William L. Dade, 11; Carl W. Riley, 8; and Owen Gowans, 7.

THE PHILADELPHIA INQUIRER / EDWARD J. FREEMAN

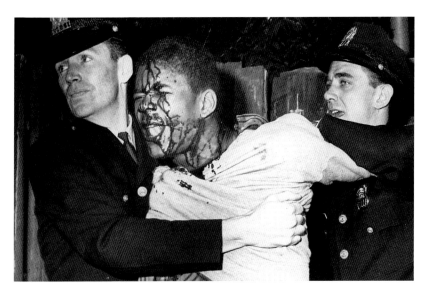

**An injured NAACP demonstrator** is restrained at a school construction site in Strawberry Mansion. Jobs for blacks in the construction industry were unobtainable in 1963.

THE PHILADELPHIA INQUIRER / JOSEPH CONLEY

**1971 hippies:** Make love, not war.

THE PHILADELPHIA INQUIRER / MICHAEL VIOLA

**Many anti-war demonstrations** took place on Independence Mall in the late 1960s and '70s.

THE PHILADELPHIA INQUIRER / JAMES L. McGARRITY

**Anti-Vietnam War protesters** pour animal blood at an Air Force recruiting station at Broad and Cherry Streets in 1972.

THE PHILADELPHIA INQUIRER / RUSSELL SALMON

**A protester against
the Vietnam War**
is hauled away by
Philadelphia police.

**Gay rights became a cause** in the last quarter of the century, as activists like Tracy Sandberg and Jamie Swidler of the Gay and Lesbian Task Force, shown at a 1987 local rally, demanded equal treatment for homosexuals. The gay-rights movement began after the Stonewall riots of June 1969, when New York police clashed with patrons of a gay bar in Greenwich Village. The riots gave rise to the belief that gay people should fight back when discriminated against.

THE PHILADELPHIA INQUIRER / REBECCA BARGER

**In the late 1960s, young gang members** were terrorizing black neighborhoods. To redeem them from the streets, Sister Falaka Fattah in 1968 organized the House of Umoja, a settlement house/ training school in West Philadelphia.

THE PHILADELPHIA INQUIRER / WILLIAM F. STEINMETZ

**It was not just young people** demanding to be heard. In 1970, Maggie Kuhn of Germantown founded the Gray Panthers to promote elder power.

THE PHILADELPHIA INQUIRER / JOSEPH J. CONLEY

**The 1992 opening of United Bank of Philadelphia** gave African Americans their first black-controlled bank in decades. Founder and CEO Emma Chappell, who was national treasurer of Jesse Jackson's 1984 presidential campaign, is joined by Jackson at the bank's grand opening.

**Passersby step around** a "die-in" protesting U.S. actions in the Persian Gulf War, 1990. THE PHILADELPHIA INQUIRER / ED HILLE

**Anti-Vietnam War** protest, 1972. THE PHILADELPHIA INQUIRER / MICHAEL VIOLA

**The Berrigan brothers,** Philip and Daniel, were Catholic peace activists put on trial in Montgomery County Court in 1981 for splattering blood and smashing nose cones for missiles at a General Electric facility in King of Prussia. They were convicted and jailed.

THE PHILADELPHIA INQUIRER / MICHAEL VIOLA

# The Bad Old Days

**F**ROM THE JEWISH AND IRISH MOBS that controlled the rackets and corrupted the political process before and immediately after Prohibition to the Italian and African-American gangs of a later era, the City of Brotherly Love spawned a diverse cast of criminals over the last 100 years.

Organized and disorganized, ethnic and parochial, these wiseguys and wannabes helped shape the dark side of the city's character.

And while cops and prosecutors gave chase, the populace looked on — at times outraged, but more typically bemused by the ebb and flow of law and order in a city that all too often lived up to its reputation as "corrupt and contented."

Adding to the mystique of the local underworld were cameo appearances by such national figures as Al Capone, arrested

**Repeal of Prohibition,** Dec. 5, 1933.

here in 1929, and Willie Sutton, the notorious bank robber. Sutton, like Capone, ended up as a guest at the imposing Eastern State Penitentiary, whose 45-foot stone walls cast a dark shadow over the neighborhood around 22nd and Fairmount. Also part of the mix were biker gangs, the Pagans and the Warlocks, and a string of wacko/fetish murderers, like Joseph Kallinger, Gary Heidnik, and Harrison "Marty" Graham.

**Liquor seized during Prohibition** is guarded by a police officer in Camden, N.J., in 1920. TEMPLE URBAN ARCHIVES / EVENING BULLETIN

One of the first serious attempts at reform was launched in the mid-1920s, when a brigadier general on leave from the Marine Corps was brought in as public safety director. With a name that fit his mission, Smedley Darlington Butler spent two years banging his head against a wall of indifference and backroom political machinations as he tried to enforce Prohibition laws, stem prostitution, and bring the rackets under control.

What he was up against was evident in the judicial system's treatment of Max "Boo Boo" Hoff, so-called "King of the Bootleggers." A grand jury investigated Hoff but failed to bring any charges, despite testimony that Hoff was in the habit of purchasing machine guns and bulletproof vests and had more than 175 telephones.

Hoff and Harry "Nig Rosen" Stromberg were major Jewish mob bosses. Their underworld ties went straight to Meyer Lansky, one of the founders of the national crime syndicate. Hoff's gang battled with several Irish and Italian gangs for control of the bootleg liquor trade and the numbers, loan-sharking, and gambling rackets.

By the 1930s, Italian-American mobsters were muscling in. Dominating that group in the '30s were the notorious Lanzetti brothers, Teo, Ignatius, Lucien, Willie, Pius and Leo. Three were killed gangland-style, as was a chief rival, John "Big Nose" Avena. Those underworld battles left at least 25 mobsters dead.

It was an unsuccessful attempt to end that type of violence, and the unwanted publicity it brought, that led to the first national mob syndicate meeting, held in Atlantic City in May 1929. On the agenda was Capone's bankrolling of Moses Annenberg's new national racing wire and a plan for mobsters to recognize each other's "rights" and cooperate if possible.

On the way back from Atlantic City, Capone, who was trying to duck hitmen from Chicago rival George "Bugs" Moran, allowed himself to be arrested in Philadelphia on a gun charge. Scarface served 10

**Al Capone** spent 10 months inside the city's Eastern State Penitentiary.

INQUIRER ARCHIVES / ASSOCIATED PRESS

months at Eastern State, where he had a lavish cell and unlimited access to the warden's phone.

By the middle of the century, the American Mafia – soon identified by its proper name, Cosa Nostra – began to dominate. Angelo Bruno, who emerged as the city's mob boss in 1959, ruled for 21 years, overseeing a relatively peaceful period in which murder was a negotiating tool of last resort. The emphasis was on making money, not headlines.

Bruno's reign ended abruptly on March 21, 1980, with a shotgun blast to the back of his head. Don Angelo was targeted by members of his own organization because of his reluctance to move in on casino gambling in Atlantic City and his refusal to engage in the drug trade. His murder sent the crime family into a spiral of violence, treachery, and betrayal that decimated the organization.

Over the next 15 years, murders and prosecutions, often based on turncoat testimony, eliminated a generation of potential leaders. Omerta, the once-sacrosanct code of silence, was now like the Liberty Bell – cracked and inoperative.

Bruno's successor, Philip "Chicken Man" Testa, was killed in a bomb blast at his home near 21st and Porter. Testa's ally, Nicodemo "Little Nicky" Scarfo, took over and used murder as a calling card. His six-year tenure was marked by the deaths of nearly 25 mobsters and ended with prosecutions and convictions of the entire hierarchy.

John Stanfa, who drove Bruno the night he was killed, took over the family in 1991 but brought even less sophistication to the job. He and two dozen top associates were arrested in 1994, convicted, and sentenced to long jail terms. The Stanfa prosecution was built around 2,000 conversations the FBI secretly recorded over two years from bugs planted in the Camden office of Stanfa's defense attorney. The lawyer was Salvatore Avena, son of John "Big Nose" Avena, Philadelphia's 1930s rackets boss. ∎

**Max "Boo Boo" Hoff** (in bow tie)
faced counterfeiting charges
in federal court in 1934.

**The United States Coast Guard** inspects a rum-running vessel off Ocean City, N.J., in 1933. INQUIRER ARCHIVES

**Revenue agents collected evidence** of illegal liquor sales by talking their way into speakeasies and surreptitiously pouring the contraband into hidden flasks.

TEMPLE URBAN ARCHIVES /
THE EVENING BULLETIN

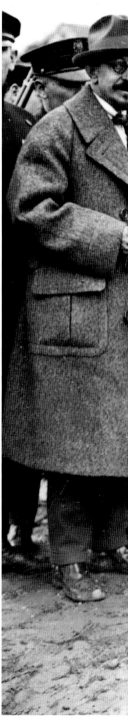

**Gen. Smedley Darlington Butler** of the U.S. Marine Corps (pointing) was recruited by Mayor W. Freeland Kendrick in 1924 to clean up the rackets. He tried but lasted only two years as public safety director due to political pressure for police to lay off. TEMPLE URBAN ARCHIVES

**The Arsenic Gang**
was linked to a series of murders in the 1930s in which victims were poisoned or drowned and their life insurance collected. More than 100 people died in the scheme. Twenty-four people were indicted, two of whom went to the electric chair; 12 others got life sentences. Shown here are five of the defendants.

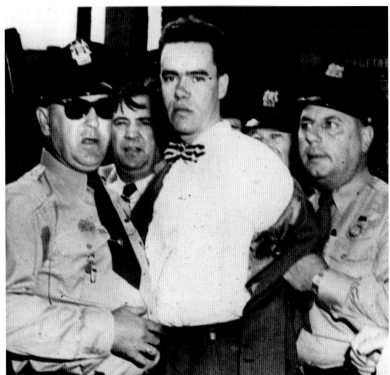

**This is the crime scene in Camden, N.J.,** after Howard Unruh went on a shooting rampage in 1949, killing 13 people and wounding three others. He was declared incompetent and incarcerated at Trenton State Hospital. INQUIRER ARCHIVES

**Notorious bank robber Willie Sutton** had a Philadelphia connection. Arrested for the attempted robbery of the Corn Exchange Bank at 60th and Ludlow Streets, he was convicted in February 1934 and sentenced to a long prison term at Eastern State Penitentiary. He and 12 other inmates broke out in 1945 by tunneling under the eight-foot-thick prison walls but were quickly rearrested. THE PHILADELPHIA INQUIRER / JOSEPH T. MARTIN

# MADMAN SPLITS SKULLS OF THREE WITH BROADAX

## Crazed Cabinet Maker Attacks Sleeping Wife and Two Others

### SMALL HOPE HELD FOR RECOVERY OF VICTIMS

Wilmington Maniac Subdued After Battle With Man He Had Brained. Begs for Death

Special to The Inquirer.

WILMINGTON, Del., Sept. 9.—Crazed from some unknown cause, Pearson Talley, 65 years old, a cabinet maker, living at No. 402 West Sixth street, this morning split open the heads of his wife, his daughter, Edith Johnson.

**Gruesome crimes and sensational headlines** were standard fare of early Philadelphia journalism. Typical of the lurid crime news is this front-page story from 1908, which recounts a bloody attack in Wilmington.

**Pius Lanzetti** had his rival, John "Big Nose" Avena, killed. A few months later, Pius was gunned down, on New Year's Eve 1936.

**Ignatius Lanzetti** saw three of his brothers meet violent deaths by 1939.

**Mickey Duffy, Irish mobster** and beer baron, was a major figure in the 1920s underworld, involved in bootlegging liquor and racketeering. Duffy lived ostentatiously in the "Black Palm Castle" on City Avenue, a place of sumptuous luxury. Duffy was gunned down in an Atlantic City hotel room in 1931, apparently betrayed by his own bodyguards.

INQUIRER ARCHIVES

**The Lanzetti gang** — six brothers from South Philadelphia — left their mark on the underworld in the 1930s. Dealers in dope, prostitution, numbers, and bootleg liquor, three of the six — Willie, Pius and Leo — were killed in gang warfare. Willie (left with hand to mouth) and Lucien (right with hand to mouth) are shown at a 1933 hearing on charges of operating a numbers bank. TEMPLE URBAN ARCHIVES

**Police remove the body of Willie Lanzetti,** carefully sewn into a burlap bag, from the underbrush in Wynnewood, Pa., following his 1939 gangland slaying. He left town after the 1936 murder of his brother Pius but made the mistake of coming back. TEMPLE URBAN ARCHIVES

# 3 LANZETTIS FACE QUIZ IN MURDER
NOV 7 - 1935

Brothers and 2 Other Men in Bail 'To Appear When Wanted' in Gabriel Killing

## HIS WIDOW AT HEARING

Mrs. Joseph Gabriel    Teo Lanzetti

Three of the notorious Lanzetti brothers and two other men were held in $5,000 bail each today by Magistrate O'Malley "to appear when wanted," in connection with the murder of Joseph Gabriel.

**Mob boss Angelo Bruno** (right) and underboss Philip "Chicken Man" Testa arrive for a hearing at the police station at 11th and Wharton Streets in 1968. THE PHILADELPHIA INQUIRER / JOSEPH CONLEY

**Bruno, gunned down** in front of his South Philadelphia home near 10th and Snyder, had been Philadelphia mob boss for two decades until his murder on March 21, 1980. The hit led to 15 years of violence, prosecutions, and turncoat testimony. THE PHILADELPHIA INQUIRER / GERARD C. BENENE

**One year after Bruno was killed,** his successor, Philip Testa, died in a bomb blast on his front porch at Porter Street near 21st.

THE PHILADELPHIA INQUIRER / VICKI VALERIO

**John Stanfa** was driving the car in which Angelo Bruno was shot. He took over the crime family in 1991, was arrested in 1994, and is serving five consecutive life terms.

THE PHILADELPHIA INQUIRER / GERALD S. WILLIAMS

**Since Angelo Bruno's death,** more than 40 Philadelphia mobsters have been murdered, including:

| **John Simone** | **Frank Sindone** | **Frank "Chickie" Narducci** | **Frank Monte** | **Salvatore Testa** | **"Frankie Flowers" D'Alfo** |
| Shot in 1980 | Shot in 1980 | Shot in 1982 | Shot in 1982 | Shot in 1984 | Shot in 1985 |

**Nicodemo "Little Nicky" Scarfo** took control of the local mob after Testa's 1981 death. Scarfo's brutal reign lasted until 1987, when he was arrested and later tried on racketeering and murder charges. He is in a federal prison in Atlanta, serving consecutive 14- and 55-year terms.

THE PHILADELPHIA INQUIRER / CLEM MURRAY

**Mario Riccobene**
Shot in 1993

**Michael Ciancaglini**
Shot in 1993

**A group headed by reputed boss Joseph "Skinny Joey" Merlino** allegedly continued to exercise some control. Authorities say the group had formed a alliance with the Pagans motorcycle gang and with some African American gangs. Merlino was jailed in 1999.

PHILADELPHIA DAILY NEWS / YONG KIM

**Angelo Bruno shared the spotlight briefly with the Black Mafia,** a street gang based around 20th and Carpenter that, through threats of violence and extortion, attempted to control gambling, prostitution, and drug-dealing in black neighborhoods. One of the leaders was Major Benjamin Coxson, whose flamboyant wardrobe and penchant for expensive automobiles turned him into one of the area's first celebrity gangsters. Coxson was found shot to death, gangland-style, in his lavish Cherry Hill, N.J., home in 1973.

THE PHILADELPHIA INQUIRER / ALEXANDER McCAUGHEY

**Samuel "Big Sam" Christian,** another of the original leaders of the Black Mafia.

INQUIRER ARCHIVES

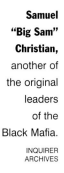

**Ira Einhorn,** guru of the counterculture in the 1960s, went on the run after being charged with the 1977 murder of his lover, Holly Maddux. Her body, stuffed in a trunk, is being removed from Einhorn's Powelton Village apartment.

THE PHILADELPHIA INQUIRER / SHARON J. WOHLMUTH

**Einhorn in 1979** with defense attorney Arlen Specter. Convicted of murder in absentia, Einhorn was tracked down in southern France in 1998 but fought extradition. He was ultimately brought back to Pennsylvania in 2001 and is serving a life sentence. THE PHILADELPHIA INQUIRER / EDWARD J. FREEMAN

**Former Upper Merion High School teacher William Bradfield** is led to a hearing in Harrisburg, Pa., in 1983. Bradfield was convicted of the 1979 murder of his fellow teacher, Susan Reinert. Her two children, Michael and Karen, have never been found. THE PHILADELPHIA INQUIRER / NICK KELSH (LEFT); UPI (TOP)

**The conviction of Mumia Abu-Jamal** for the 1981 murder of Philadelphia Police Officer Daniel Faulkner became an international cause celebre. The former radio reporter rallied worldwide support by claiming he was a victim of racism. Law-enforcement advocates describe him as a cop-killer who has manipulated the media.

PHILADELPHIA DAILY NEWS / SAM PSORAS

**Sylvia Seegrist,** who killed three people in a shooting spree at the Springfield Mall in 1985, is brought in for a hearing in Delaware County.
THE PHILADELPHIA INQUIRER / ED HILLE

**On Feb. 26, 1981, Joey Coyle** of South Philadelphia found a pile of money that had fallen out of an armored truck, and it turned his life around — but not for the better. The FBI nailed him at the airport with some of the money and a one-way ticket to Acapulco. Twelve years later, the guy who once had $1.2 million was found at home hanging by an electrical cord. A movie, *Money for Nothing*, starring John Cusack, was made in 1993.
THE PHILADELPHIA INQUIRER

**Joseph Kallinger,** a Kensington shoemaker, went on a sex and killing spree in 1973. Convicted in 1974 of killing his son and another boy, he received two life sentences, then was convicted of other sex murders. INQUIRER ARCHIVES / ASSOCIATED PRESS

**Philadelphia's own odd couple:** Gary Heidnik (left) and Marty Graham, leaving a court hearing in 1988. Both were convicted of grisly murders, involving sex slaves and torture. Heidnik was convicted of 18 counts, including first-degree murder, rape, kidnapping of two women, and enslavement of four others in the basement of his North Philadelphia rowhouse. He was executed in 1999. Graham received six death sentences and one life sentence for the murders of seven women.
INQUIRER ARCHIVES / ASSOCIATED PRESS

# Great Moments in Sports

SPORTS MANIA GRIPS PHILADELPHIA as the 20th century ends. Nearly all the 339 games played each year by the four major professional teams are televised. Some radio and TV stations devote their days entirely to sports and sports talk. New football and baseball stadiums are in the works.

Yet in terms of overall significance in American sports, Philadelphia in the final years of the 20th century can't match the big events and glorious successes that marked the early decades.

Wilt Chamberlain, Tom Gola, Jack Dempsey, Joe Frazier, Bill Tilden, Steve Van Buren, Bobby Jones, Mike Schmidt — all had their historic moments here. Connie Mack managed the Philadelphia A's for more than 50 years. Eddie Gottlieb, a South Philly hustler, helped create a new basketball

**Running back Steve Van Buren** led the Eagles to consecutive league championships in 1948 and 1949.
THE PHILADELPHIA INQUIRER

league after World War II, the NBA. The Big Five carved a niche for itself in college basketball.

The gentlemanly Mack came to Philadelphia with the new century, arriving in 1900 to form the Athletics, a keystone franchise in Ban Johnson's brand-new American League. Mack's eye for talent soon made the A's a power and helped turn Philadelphia into baseball's capital. They won the World Series in 1910, '11, '13, '29, and '30 with such stars as Rube Waddell, Frank "Home Run" Baker, Jimmie Foxx, and Lefty Grove. Their ballpark at 21st and Lehigh, Shibe Park, was the first modern stadium when it opened in 1909. The Reach Sporting

**Connie Mack's Philadelphia Athletics** dominated the city's sporting life through the first half of the century. Twice, from 1910 through 1914 and again from 1929 through 1931, the A's were baseball's dominant team. But the frugal Mack, their owner-manager, dismantled both teams by selling off their stars. Here, the world-champion A's of 1911 surround Mack and Louis Van Zelst, their bat boy and mascot.
THE PHILADELPHIA INQUIRER

Goods Co. of Fishtown manufactured the big leagues' baseballs, and the *Sporting Life*, a locally produced weekly, chronicled the game for an eager city.

By contrast, the National League's Phillies, two decades older than the A's, won just two pennants and a single World Series game in the century's first 50 years. It wasn't until 1980, nine years after they had abandoned renamed Connie Mack Stadium for Veterans Stadium, that the Phils won their first and only World Series. The stars of the great Phillies teams of the late 1970s and early '80s included Larry Bowa, Garry Maddox, Pete Rose, Mike Schmidt, and Steve Carlton.

That year of 1980 was the high-water mark for Philadelphia's pro teams. All four — Phillies, Eagles, 76ers, and Flyers — reached the championship round, though only Dallas Green's Phillies won.

The Eagles, NFL descendants of the Frankford Yellowjackets, won three league titles between 1948 and 1960. The powerful legs of running back Steve Van Buren brought them the first two, in 1948 and 1949. By 1960, with the NFL making serious claims on America's sports consciousness, the Eagles turned to the air. The dynamic combination of quarterback Norm Van Brocklin and flanker Tommy McDonald, both Hall of Famers, led the 1960 Eagles to the championship.

Dick Vermeil coached the 1980 Eagles, with Bill Bergey and Wilbert Montgomery, to a memorable NFC championship game win over hated Dallas. But the Oakland Raiders dominated the Eagles in Super Bowl XV. The Birds returned to the big game in 2005, losing to the New England Patriots in Super Bowl XXXIX.

College football's golden age in Philadelphia ended in the 1950s when Penn joined the Ivy League and deemphasized sports. The Quakers frequently led the nation in attendance and won national titles in 1904 and 1908.

Another Philadelphia tradition is the annual Army-Navy game, a rivalry that since 1893 has been played in Philadelphia, with a few exceptions, because it is midway between the two military academies.

College basketball has had a long run of success in the city. The 1954 LaSalle Explorers, with Olney-born all-American Tom Gola, won the NCAA championship. Penn, Temple, and St. Joseph's all reached Final Fours before the Big Five's fifth member, Villanova, captured another NCAA title in 1985.

Villanova also made local track and field history under James Francis "Jumbo" Elliott, who ruled a dynasty that produced 21 Olympians. Elliott's runners often dominated the Penn Relays, the nation's premier track and field festival since 1895.

**Grover Cleveland Alexander** was a gifted pitcher for the Phillies from 1911 to 1917. He won 190 games here and led the Phils to their first pennant in 1915. INQUIRER ARCHIVES

The Philadelphia area has produced an extraordinary number of boxers – from Tommy Loughran to Harold Johnson to Joey Giardello to Bennie Briscoe to Joe Frazier to Matthew Saad Muhammad – but the city's prominence in the sport faded when Las Vegas became the big-fight mecca.

Rowing on the Schuylkill, immortalized in the paintings of Thomas Eakins, continues to be a popular sport. The annual Dad Vail Regatta brings thousands of college rowers to the river each spring. Boathouse Row has produced dozens of Olympians, the most noteworthy of whom was Jack Kelly Sr., father of actress Grace Kelly.

Bill Tilden, son of a Germantown merchant, in the 1920s became the greatest American tennis player. He won seven U.S. Opens, including six in a row, 1920-25.

Maybe the most dramatic moment in the region's sporting history occurred on a September day in 1930 at the Merion Cricket Club. There, followed by an enormous gallery and guarded by state policemen, Bobby Jones won the U.S. Amateur, becoming the only golfer ever to win the game's Grand Slam. ∎

**When it opened in 1909, Shibe Park,** at 21st and Lehigh, was the first modern, concrete-and-steel stadium (shown in 1948). It was the Athletics' home until they moved to Kansas City in 1954. The Phillies moved here in 1938. They remained at the renamed Connie Mack Stadium through 1970. THE PHILADELPHIA INQUIRER

**Eddie Collins** was near the end of his career when he returned to Philadelphia for the 1927 season.

**The great A's teams of the late 1920s** included several future Hall of Famers, some of whom — like the aging Tris Speaker, Eddie Collins, and Ty Cobb (from left, shown in 1927) — played here only briefly. These veterans joined an A's team that soon would win three straight pennants (1929-31) with youthful stars like Lefty Grove and Jimmie Foxx.

**Excitement over the 1929 World Series** between the A's and Joe McCarthy's Chicago Cubs was so high that Shibe Park's 20th Street neighbors turned their rooftops into grandstands. The practice became commonplace until the A's in 1935 constructed a 50-foot-high tin wall, which quickly became known as the "Spite Fence." The A's defeated the Cubs in five games in the '29 Series, for the fourth of five championships they would win in Philadelphia.

INQUIRER ARCHIVES

**While the Phillies have won just one World Series** in their long history, they have been blessed with several Hall of Famers. One of the greatest was Chuck Klein, an outfielder who, despite playing on a seventh-place team in 1933, won the National League Triple Crown with 28 homers, 120 RBIs, and a .368 batting average. THE PHILADELPHIA INQUIRER

**The two great stars of the A's 1929-31 pennant winners** were pitcher Lefty Grove (above) and slugging first baseman Jimmie Foxx. Signed by Connie Mack out of small towns in Maryland, they eventually were sold in moves that triggered the Athletics' descent into the second division.

INQUIRER ARCHIVES

**The perfect game:** Phillies pitcher Jim Bunning strikes out the Mets' John Stephenson on June 21, 1964, to finish the National League's first perfect game of the 20th century. It was the highlight of a cursed Phils' season. Leading the league by 6½ games with 12 to play, Gene Mauch's club lost 10 in a row in one of baseball's most memorable collapses. INQUIRER ARCHIVES / UNITED PRESS INTERNATIONAL

**The greatest era in Phillies history** took place between 1975 and 1983, when the team won five division titles, two pennants, and its only world championship, in 1980. In that stretch, the club featured the pitching of Steve Carlton, the power of Mike Schmidt, and, for four years anyway, the leadership of Pete Rose. In 1981, Rose (above) broke Stan Musial's NL hit record. THE PHILADELPHIA INQUIRER / GERALD S. WILLIAMS

**Phillies slugger Mike Schmidt** slaps his hands after hitting his 500th home run on April 18, 1987. Schmidt, who is considered among the game's greatest third basemon, won the league's Most Valuable Player award three times. He hit 30 or more home runs in 13 seasons.

THE PHILADELPHIA INQUIRER / JOHN SLEEZER

**Hall of Fame** pitcher Steve Carlton played for the Phillies from 1972 to '86. He won the Cy Young award four times while here.

THE PHILADELPHIA INQUIRER / CLEM MURRAY

**One of the lasting images of the Phillies'** 1980 World Series victory over the Kansas City Royals came after the final out of Game 6 when Series MVP Mike Schmidt leaped into the arms of closer Tug McGraw — very much out of character for the introspective third baseman.

THE PHILADELPHIA INQUIRER / CHARLES ISAACS

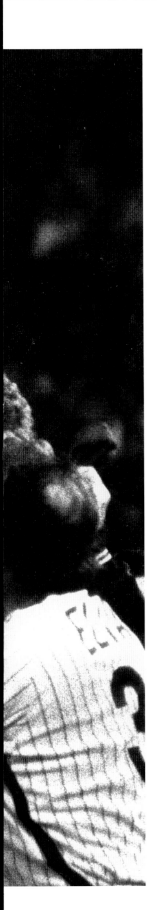

**John Kruk,** the beer-bellied epitome of the Phillies' 1993 NL champions, scores the winning run in Game 1 of their League Championship Series triumph over the heavily favored Atlanta Braves. Philadelphians bonded with that blue-collar team, which lost the World Series to Toronto on Joe Carter's home run off Mitch Williams. Lenny Dykstra, arms raised, and Darren Daulton greet Kruk. THE PHILADELPHIA INQUIRER / RON CORTES

**The leader of the 1993 Phillies** was their talented catcher, Darren Daulton. THE PHILADELPHIA INQUIRER / JERRY LODRIGUSS

Pennsylvania's restrictive Blue Laws prohibited Sunday sporting events until the 1930s. The Eagles, who had begun existence as the Frankford Yellowjackets, played their first Sunday game at Shibe Park on Nov. 12, 1933.

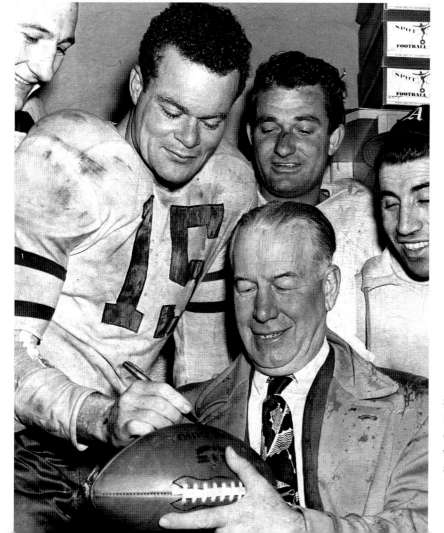

**Steve Van Buren** autographs a football for his coach, Earle "Greasy" Neale, after the Eagles won the first of two consecutive NFL championships in 1948 with a 7-0 victory over the Chicago Cardinals at Shibe Park. THE PHILADELPHIA INQUIRER / FORREST SMITH

**The Eagles' 1948 championship-game win** over the Cardinals took place in near-blizzard conditions. Before the game, which started 30 minutes late, players from both teams helped clear Shibe Park's playing surface with shovels. The only touchdown came on Steve Van Buren's five-yard run early in the fourth quarter. THE PHILADELPHIA INQUIRER / HAROLD CARTER

**The Eagles won the NFL championship** in 1960, when they beat Vince Lombardi's Green Bay Packers, 17-13, at Franklin Field. Here, wide receiver Tommy McDonald is helped to his feet after scoring a touchdown on a pass from Norm Van Brocklin. Both men ended up in the Pro Football Hall of Fame. INQUIRER ARCHIVES

**By 1963, Norm Van Brocklin** (above) had retired and the Eagles' record had fallen to 2-10-2. Still, they remained a potent offensive team. From left: Quarterback Sonny Jurgensen could call on tight end Pete Retzlaff, running back Timmy Brown, or flanker Tommy McDonald. After that season, Jurgensen was traded to Washington and McDonald to Dallas.

THE PHILADELPHIA INQUIRER / ROBERT L. MOONEY

**The spiritual leader of the 1960 Eagles** was Chuck Bednarik. A Bethlehem-born all-American at Penn, Bednarik, a center and linebacker, was the last of the NFL's two-way players and was feared throughout the league.

**Coach Dick Vermeil** led the Eagles to their first Super Bowl appearance in 1981. Owner Leonard Tose hired Vermeil after watching him guide UCLA to a Rose Bowl victory. Here, Vermeil is carried off Veterans Stadium's frozen turf by defensive linemen Carl Hairston (left) and Claude Humphrey after the Eagles defeated Dallas in the NFC championship game. THE PHILADELPHIA INQUIRER / CLEM MURRAY

**Middle linebacker Bill Bergey,** whose beard lent him the ominous look of a movie villain, was the heart of the Eagles defense that championship season.

**As starting quarterback for Dick Vermeil's Eagles, Ron Jaworski** led the Birds to the playoffs four times and to the edge of glory in Super Bowl XV in 1981. In his 10 years with the Eagles, Jaworski compiled impressive stats, including 116 consecutive regular-season starts.

**By the late 1980s,** the grunt-and-grind football epitomized by Bednarik and Bergey had given way to a faster, more athletic game. Randall Cunningham was the prototype of the new NFL quarterback. Fast and elusive, Cunningham often seemed to defy gravity during several seasons with Buddy Ryan's Eagles.

THE PHILADELPHIA INQUIRER / ED HILLE

**One of the favorite receivers** for both Jaworski and Cunningham was Mike Quick, the team's No. 1 draft choice in 1982 and now an Eagles radio broadcaster.

THE PHILADELPHIA INQUIRER / JERRY LODRIGUSS

**In one of the most bizarre playoff games ever,** the Chicago Bears defeated the Eagles, 20-12, on Dec. 29, 1988. The plays were so obscured at the "Fog Bowl" in Soldier Field that even the coaches on the sidelines had difficulty following the action. THE PHILADELPHIA INQUIRER / MICHAEL BRYANT

**Eagles coach Buddy Ryan,** who generated unprecedented passion in Philadelphia's fans, had a definite defensive bias. He is shown in 1988 with three members of the great defense he put together — end Reggie White (center), tackle Jerome Brown (No. 99) and linebacker Todd Bell (left). Brown, one of the game's rising stars, was killed in a Florida auto accident in 1992. White died in 2004.

THE PHILADELPHIA INQUIRER / VICKI VALERIO

A couple of hundred miles to the northwest of Philadelphia, Joe Paterno has built one of the nation's outstanding collegiate programs at Penn State. Paterno has been the Nittany Lions' head coach since 1966, leading them to national championships in 1982 and 1986.

THE PHILADELPHIA INQUIRER / CLEM MURRAY

**Philadelphia today is not known as a college-football town,** but at one time the annual Army-Navy game attracted more than 100,000 fans to old Municipal Stadium in South Philadelphia. THE PHILADELPHIA INQUIRER

**Until the 1950s,** the University of Pennsylvania's football teams were among the nation's elite, filling Franklin Field on fall Saturdays. A second deck had to be added to the campus stadium, shown in 1920, to accommodate the crowds.

**Wilt Chamberlain,** one of the greatest basketball players ever, shown vying with his nemesis, the Boston Celtics' Bill Russell. Chamberlain, an Overbrook High grad who played with the Philadelphia Warriors and 76ers, once scored a record 100 points in a single game and averaged 50 points a game for an entire NBA season (1962). Yet only once — in 1967 — could his Philadelphia teams defeat Russell's Celtics and win an NBA title.

THE PHILADELPHIA INQUIRER

**Guard Hal Greer** was one of Chamberlain's most valuable teammates on the championship 1967 Sixers squad. THE PHILADELPHIA INQUIRER / MICHAEL VIOLA

**Tom Gola,** a four-time all-American at LaSalle, was the first draft choice of Philadelphia Warriors owner Eddie Gottlieb in 1955. The Warriors moved to San Francisco and were replaced in 1963 by the 76ers, who relocated from Syracuse. THE PHILADELPHIA INQUIRER / JOSEPH CONLEY

**Billy Cunningham,** a star with the 76ers, injured his knee in a 1975 fall at the Spectrum. Once known as the "Kangaroo Kid," he never regained his leaping ability and later switched to coaching. He guided the 1983 Sixers to a world championship. THE PHILADELPHIA INQUIRER / GERARD C. BENENE

**Julius Erving — "Dr. J" —** was the star of the '83 NBA champion Sixers and a pivotal figure in the rise of the league to international prominence. He revolutionized the sport with his midair dramatics and, with Boston's Larry Bird, made the Sixers-Celtics rivalry one of the most intense in sports.

THE PHILADELPHIA INQUIRER / JOHN PAUL FILO

THE PHILADELPHIA INQUIRER

**Jubilant fans cheer** the 1983 champion 76ers during the parade down Broad Street. THE PHILADELPHIA INQUIRER

**Despite the presence of superstar Charles Barkley,** the Sixers were ousted from the 1991 NBA playoffs by Michael Jordan and his Chicago Bulls, which became the league's dominant team. Barkley was traded to Phoenix in 1992. THE PHILADELPHIA INQUIRER / JERRY LODRIGUSS

*Great Moments in Sports* **251**

**Villanova's Rollie Massimino** was a controversial figure who led the Wildcats to the 1985 NCAA championship. In a 1991 Villanova-Syracuse game, he can't believe the ref's call. THE PHILADELPHIA INQUIRER / JERRY LODRIGUSS

**Two of the stars** of Villanova's 1985 championship team, Ed Pinckney (left) and Gary McClain, celebrate on the floor of Rupp Arena after the Wildcats stunned No. 1 Georgetown in one of the most memorable NCAA title games in history. Playing a near-perfect game against Patrick Ewing's Hoyas, Villanova hit 90 percent of its shots in the second half to win, 66-64.

THE PHILADELPHIA INQUIRER / CLEM MURRAY

**The historic Palestra** and the unique Big Five have given Philadelphia a prominent place in the history of college basketball. So have the area's outstanding coaches — Jack Ramsay, Jack Kraft, Harry Litwack, Ken Loeffler, Chuck Daly. John Chaney (above), a native Philadelphian, was one of the most successful, compiling a 499-238 record at Temple before retiring in 2006. THE PHILADELPHIA INQUIRER / JERRY LODRIGUSS

**The "Broad Street Bullies,"** the successful and wildly popular Philadelphia Flyers teams of the mid-1970s, sparked a sports comeback in the city that culminated in 1980, when all four professional teams played in their sports' championships. The brawling Flyers, shown here in a 1973 battle with the California Seals at the Spectrum, won consecutive Stanley Cups in 1974 and 1975. THE PHILADELPHIA INQUIRER

**The lucky charm for those Flyers** was a recording of "God Bless America" sung by Kate Smith. When it was played at the Spectrum, the Flyers almost never lost. She occasionally performed in person, here before the Flyers won the last game in the 1974 Stanley Cup finals against Boston.

THE PHILADELPHIA INQUIRER

**The mastermind behind those great Flyers teams** was coach Fred Shero, an enigmatic leader who loved inspirational slogans and whose cerebral style often baffled his players. In seven seasons, Shero's Flyers won 64 percent of their games.

THE PHILADELPHIA INQUIRER

**The highlight of Flyers history** occurred on May 19, 1974, when they defeated the heavily favored Boston Bruins to become the first expansion team to win a Stanley Cup. Here, the team's two stars, captain Bobby Clarke and goalie Bernie Parent, hoist the Cup during the Spectrum celebration that followed their 1-0 victory over Bobby Orr's Bruins in Game 6.

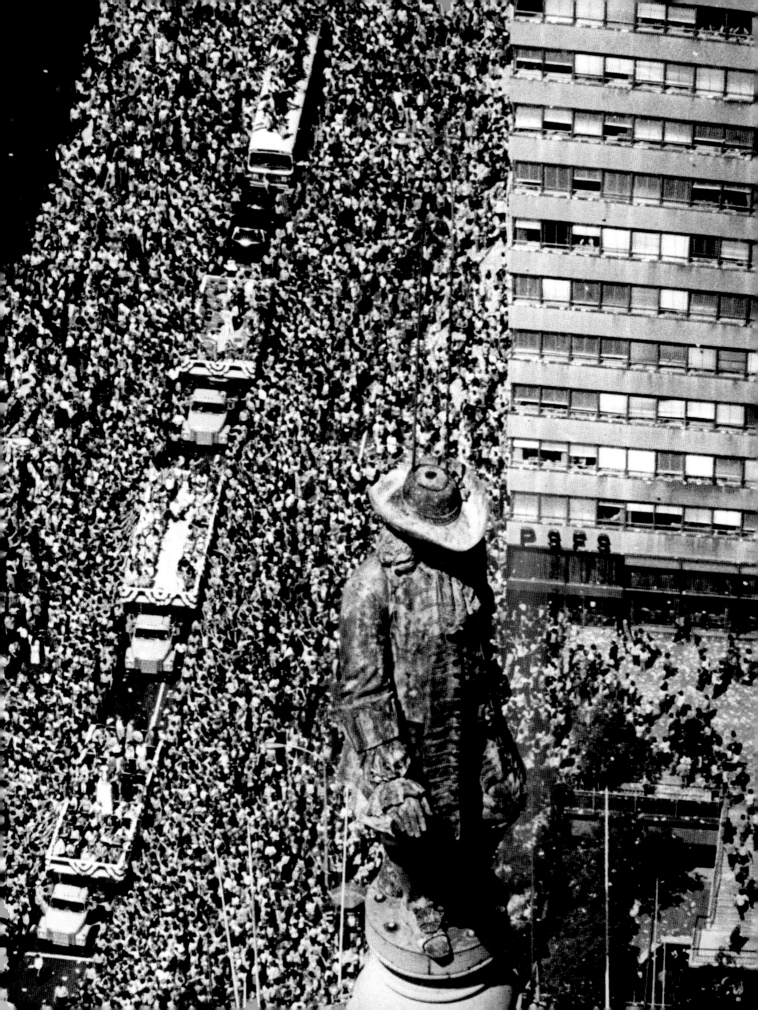

**Before the Flyers were founded in 1967,** there were a number of professional hockey teams in the city. The Philadelphia Quakers averaged fewer than 2,500 fans and won only four of 44 games in their one and only NHL season, 1930-31. Many minor-league teams followed, including the Ramblers, Arrows, and Firebirds. THE PHILADELPHIA INQUIRER

**Hundreds of thousands of Philadelphians** jammed Center City in May 1975 in celebration of the Flyers' second Stanley Cup. The players are being paraded through the crowd on the backs of flatbed trucks.

THE PHILADELPHIA INQUIRER

**The largest and most controversial transaction** in Flyers history occurred in 1992 when, after a protracted battle with the Rangers, they acquired the rights to Eric Lindros from Quebec. The explosive line of Lindros, John LeClair, and Mikael Renberg became known as the "Legion of Doom." THE PHILADELPHIA INQUIRER / JERRY LODRIGUSS

**Philadelphia's link with boxing**
is a long and historic one.
On Sept. 23, 1926, at the
new Municipal Stadium in
South Philadelphia built for
that year's Sesquicentennial
celebration, heavyweights
Gene Tunney and Jack
Dempsey (facing camera)
met in the first of their
legendary title fights.
A rain-soaked crowd of
more than 120,000 saw
Tunney take Dempsey's title
with a unanimous 10-round
decision. The following year
they met in Chicago and,
thanks to the infamous
"long count," Tunney
won again.
INQUIRER ARCHIVES

**Among the most popular Philadelphia fighters** in the early decades was light-heavyweight champion Tommy Loughran, who lost a 1934 heavyweight championship fight to Primo Carnera. Here, he trains for his 1931 bout with Jack Gross. THE PHILADELPHIA INQUIRER

**"Philadelphia Jack" O'Brien** (left), a heavyweight who weighed only 165 pounds, challenged Tommy Burns in two 20-round championship bouts in 1906 and 1907. The first ended in a draw; Burns won a referee's nod in the second. INQUIRER ARCHIVES

**One of the last major outdoor championship fights** in Philadelphia took place on June 5, 1952. Camden's "Jersey Joe" Walcott (right) defeated Ezzard Charles in a unanimous 15-round decision. INQUIRER ARCHIVES / UNITED PRESS INTERNATIONAL

**The term "Philadelphia middleweight"** implies a certain gritty toughness. Among the best of the local fighters in that classification was South Philadelphia's Joey Giardello, shown defeating Dick Tiger for the title in 1963. Giardello held it two years before Tiger took back the title. INQUIRER ARCHIVES / UNITED PRESS INTERNATIONAL

**U.S. amateur boxer David Reid** was hopelessly behind the Cuban, Alfredo Duvergel, in the third — and last — round of their match at the Olympics in Atlanta on Aug. 4, 1996. Only a knockout could win it for him. Then Reid caught him with a right. When Reid saw Duvergel hit the floor, he leaped in the air, realizing he'd won the gold medal. A sportswriter who has covered boxing for 40 years said it was the single most dramatic moment he'd ever witnessed. In 1999, Reid won the WBA junior middleweight championship and was undefeated in 12 pro fights.

THE PHILADELPHIA INQUIRER / RON CORTES

**Joe Frazier,** a transplanted Philadelphian and heavyweight champion, fought Muhammad Ali in some of the most stirring battles in history. On March 8, 1971, Frazier handed Ali his first defeat with a 15-round decision at Madison Square Garden. Ali, who lived in Cherry Hill, N.J., in the 1970s, returned the favor in the memorable "Thrilla in Manila" four years later. INQUIRER ARCHIVES / UNITED PRESS INTERNATIONAL

**Carl Lewis of Willingboro, N.J.,** became one of track and field's greatest and longest-lasting stars. The winner of a record nine Olympic gold medals in sprints and the long jump, Lewis carries the flag after winning the 100 meters at the 1984 Summer Games in Los Angeles. THE PHILADELPHIA INQUIRER / JOHN PAUL FILO

**James "Jumbo" Elliott,** Villanova's legendary track coach, produced 21 Olympians and dozens of Penn Relays champions. One of the first to import athletes from overseas, Elliott coached at Villanova for 46 years, from 1935 to 1981. THE PHILADELPHIA INQUIRER

**The Penn Relays,** begun in 1895 and held each spring at Franklin Field, became the nation's most popular and significant annual track and field event. Penn's Barney Berlinger, the "King of the Decathlon," is shown winning the 110-meter hurdles at the 1931 relays. THE PHILADELPHIA INQUIRER

**Only one golfer** has ever won the sport's Grand Slam. Bobby Jones (above) completed that feat in 1930 with a victory in the U.S. Amateur at Merion Cricket Club. Another great moment: In 1950, Ben Hogan, recuperating from a near-fatal auto accident and barely able to walk through the final day's 36 holes, captured the U.S. Open at Merion. INQUIRER ARCHIVES

**Helen Sigel Wilson** was one of the nation's outstanding amateur golfers in the 1940s and '50s. Wilson, who later became a successful restaurateur, won 12 Philadelphia Amateur titles, twice was a runner-up in the U.S. Amateur, and was named captain of the Curtis Cup team in 1978. THE PHILADELPHIA INQUIRER / LARRY KEIGHLEY

**Perhaps the greatest American tennis player** of the 20th century was Philadelphia's Bill Tilden. He won seven U.S. Opens, including six in a row (1920-25), and three Wimbledon titles (1920, '21, and '30). When the greatest athletes of the first half of the century were chosen, his margin was greater than Babe Ruth's in baseball or Bobby Jones' in golf. INQUIRER ARCHIVES

**Perhaps no Philadelphia family** won fame on more fronts than the Kellys. John B. Kelly Jr. (below), the future City Council member and brother of actress Grace Kelly, was a world-class rower. His father, John B. Kelly Sr. (right), who trained on the Schuylkill and earned a fortune as a building contractor, won a gold medal in single sculls at the 1920 Olympics in Brussels.

**The CoreStates U.S. Pro Cycling Championship** began in Philadelphia in 1985. Here, Eric Heiden, who won a record five speedskating gold medals at the 1980 Winter Olympics and later excelled as a cyclist, crosses the finish line to win in 1985. PHILADELPHIA DAILY NEWS / ED CARREON

**A number of auto-racing tracks** surrounded Philadelphia. Among the most notable was the Langhorne Speedway, whose dirt oval is shown here in 1929. THE PHILADELPHIA INQUIRER

**An ironworker scales the Comcast Center,** the 57-story building that when completed would become the city's tallest. It would serve as headquarters for Comcast Corp., the cable company that was Philadelphia's fastest-growing big business at the turn of the 21st century.

# The New Millennium

THE NEW CENTURY ARRIVED with an outbreak of civic optimism. There was a growing sense that the city's story of the last 40 years — a tale of loss, decay and decline — had taken a turn for the better.

Signs of revival could be found in many neighborhoods, especially Center City. To see the change, all you had to do was try to thread through the thick crowds at midday. Even at night, the restaurants and sidewalk cafes were filled, often with the young, soaking up the urban vibes.

Construction cranes dotted the skyline as new buildings went up and old office buildings were reincarnated as condos. Vacant land went for premium prices and became new townhouses. (A townhouse is a rowhouse that costs more than $200,000.)

**Center City** had no sidewalk cafes in 1995. By 2006, there were more than 185, including this one outside Mercato. PHILADELPHIA DAILY NEWS / JESSICA GRIFFIN

There was a civic building spree, too. The Eagles and the Phillies got spanking-new stadiums, and the Philadelphia Orchestra got a new home in the Kimmel Center, an instant landmark at Broad and Spruce Streets with its distinctive glass dome.

Independence Mall, a child of the 1950s, was redone and repopulated with new buildings: a new home for the Liberty Bell, a red-brick Visitor Center and a grand exhibition center devoted to the U.S. Constitution.

The old city sported a new vibrancy, evident when the clock struck midnight on New Year's Eve of 1999 and thousands of revelers greeted the new year. The city fathers, as they always did, proudly proclaimed it the best New Year celebration ever. Philadelphians were celebrating the beginning of a new century and a new millennium — a double excuse to party.

The Philadelphia that entered the 21st century was different in so many ways from the city of 1900.

One hundred years before, the expanding city was enjoying a building boom. A new block of rowhouses had to go up every week to keep pace with the new arrivals, many of them immigrants or the children of immigrants.

The city's population had doubled from 1860 to 1890. It would double again between 1890 and 1950, topping out at close to 2.1 million.

One hundred years before, government struggled to provide the newcomers with clean water, new streets, water and sewer lines, and police service throughout an expanding city that was linked by trolley.

One hundred years later, the struggle was to manage decline. In just 40 years, beginning in the early 1960s, the city lost 500,000 residents, many fleeing to the growing suburbs. The city's biggest challenge now was keeping pace with the rate of abandonment.

One out of five lived in poverty. With poverty came crime, often related to the drug trade, and a rise in the number of homicides, often children cut down by stray bullets. The death of innocents haunted the city.

**The city's skyline,** as viewed from the Cira Centre, has been transformed by the addition of new skyscrapers.

THE PHILADELPHIA INQUIRER / PETER TOBIA

After the Civil War, Philadelphia proudly took the name Workshop of the World, to tout the machinery it manufactured so well.

By the turn of the 21st century, most of the industry was gone. For jobs, the city depended on higher education, medicine and pharmaceuticals (Eds and Meds, as they were called), on service industries (the law and accounting offices that filled the skyscrapers) and on tourism.

There was one locally owned giant of the electronic age. Comcast Corp., a small cable-TV company founded by Ralph Roberts, grew into a huge national firm — and built a taller-than-anything tower to proclaim its new status.

By American standards, Philadelphia is as ancient as Rome. In a nation where anything built before World War II is considered antique, Philadelphia has buildings that were standing before the colonies declared independence from Great Britain in 1776.

The texture, the feel, the realness of a city laid out in 1682 attracted folks from around the world, nearly 2 million strong each year, to see the Liberty Bell, Independence Hall, and Society Hill, and buy souvenirs. Odds are, those Philly mementos were made in China.

In 2000, Philadelphia was a bit player in a global economy. Most of our clothing, our furnishings, even some of our food came from overseas. The world was interconnected by air, as we learned to our horror on Sept. 11, 2001, when two airliners piloted by terrorists brought down the World Trade Center in New York City. Soon, the United States was at war in Afghanistan and Iraq, a conflict that ended up lasting for years.

New Year's Day 2000 dawned bright and clear, a good omen for the new century. The same 100 years that changed Philadelphia in so many ways left it remarkably intact. Although someone who stepped into a time machine in 1900 and was deposited onto Broad Street in 2000 would surely marvel at the changes — not to mention the traffic — familiar landmarks remained.

The city would hold many surprises for our time traveler. A majority of residents were now African American, Asian and Latino, and, astonishingly, the city was resolutely Democratic.

But wouldn't Boathouse Row look much the same? Rittenhouse Square the same? Independence Hall the same? Even City Hall, sheathed for decades in a sooty gray, had undergone a deep cleaning and emerged almost as pure and white as it was in 1900.

Over the last 100 years, the city has gone through times of trial and change, periods of optimism and pessimism, cycles of decline and revival. The revelers come and go. The city moves on. ■

**A surreal moment,** courtesy of a skater scaling the steps of the Philadelphia Museum of Art, which were plastered with a gigantic photo of Salvador Dalí. The portrait promoted an exhibit of the Spanish artist's work that drew nearly 375,000 visitors to the museum in 2005. THE PHILADELPHIA INQUIRER / PETER TOBIA

**With its computerized light shows,** architect Cesar Pelli's glass-and-steel Cira Centre illuminates the western sky. When it opened in 2006, it became the first skyscraper in the 30th Street Station area. THE PHILADELPHIA INQUIRER / BARBARA L. JOHNSTON

**In the 1990s, construction cranes returned** to Center City as developers rushed to meet a surge in demand for new apartments and condominiums. The population of downtown grew by 10,000 during the decade, and the growth continued into the new century. Some buildings were new, but most were old office buildings, reincarnated as condos selling for $500,000-plus per unit. This one, The National in Old City, features a picture-perfect view of the Benjamin Franklin Bridge. THE PHILADELPHIA INQUIRER / PETER TOBIA

**Market Street,** west of City Hall, was a thriving business district with crowds navigating the city on foot. THE PHILADELPHIA INQUIRER / CLEM MURRAY

**Slave quarters at Sixth and Market Streets,** in what was once the presidential mansion of George Washington, were discovered when the site was excavated following construction of the new Liberty Bell Center (below). Plans eventually were made to commemorate the site. In the meantime, visitors got to watch archeologists comb the remains of the mansion for artifacts.
THE PHILADELPHIA INQUIRER / AKIRA SUWA

**Workers add a stainless-steel Preamble** to the Constitution as a finishing touch to the façade of the new National Constitution Center, the museum and exhibit center that opened in 2003 on Independence Mall. The center, a favorite project of Mayor Edward G. Rendell's, soon was drawing hundreds of thousands of visitors each year. THE PHILADELPHIA INQUIRER / ERIC MENCHER

THE PHILADELPHIA INQUIRER / PETER TOBIA

**With its vaulted glass ceiling,** the Kimmel Center for the Performing Arts became an instant landmark when it opened in 2001. Opening night drew a crowd of dignitaries and performers, including (from top) violinist Itzhak Perlman, cellist Yo-Yo Ma, and the center's benefactors, Caroline and Sidney Kimmel.

**In 1993, German conductor Wolfgang Sawallisch** became the seventh music director of the Philadelphia Orchestra. He led the ensemble for 10 years, overseeing its move from the Academy of Music to its new home, Verizon Hall. THE PHILADELPHIA INQUIRER / AKIRA SUWA

**Christoph Eschenbach** succeeded Sawallisch, but his relationship with the musicians was a difficult one, and his tenure as music director lasted only five years.

**Prince Charles, accompanied by his wife,** Camilla Parker Bowles, the Duchess of Cornwall, became the first Prince of Wales to visit Philadelphia since Queen Victoria's son and heir, Edward, toured the city in 1860. Charles and Camilla attended the Academy Ball in January 2007, which marked the 150th anniversary of the Academy of Music.

The World Cafe, a concert hall named after the nationally syndicated show produced by WXPN-FM, the University of Pennsylvania's radio station, opened in 2004 as a classy new venue for rock and folk music. THE PHILADELPHIA INQUIRER / JOHN COSTELLO

M. Night Shyamalan, born in India but raised in Penn Valley, became Philadelphia's most famous movie director. The Waldron Mercy and Episcopal Academy graduate lived in Wayne and favored the region as the setting for his hit movies, which included *The Sixth Sense* and *Signs*.

THE PHILADELPHIA INQUIRER / MICHAEL BRYANT

Considered among the greatest American paintings of the 19th century, Thomas Eakins' masterpiece, *The Gross Clinic*, hung for years in a little-visited gallery at Thomas Jefferson University, owner of the work since it was completed in 1875. In 2006, Jefferson shocked the city by announcing it had quietly sold the painting for $68 million to an Arkansas museum funded by a Wal-Mart heiress. Within weeks, a local fund-raising effort was started that ultimately matched the asking price. *The Gross Clinic* stayed and was unveiled in its new home at the Philadelphia Museum of Art in 2007. THE PHILADELPHIA INQUIRER / ERIC MENCHER

**Edward G. Rendell,** Philadelphia's popular mayor through most of the 1990s — and ardent Eagles fan — was elected governor of Pennsylvania in 2002. His successor as mayor, City Council President John F. Street (below), took office in January 2000 and promptly announced a plan to remove abandoned cars from the city's streets.

**Cardinal Anthony Bevilacqua** (right) shakes hands with his successor, Archbishop Justin Rigali (center), who was installed as leader of the Roman Catholic Archdiocese of Philadelphia in a ceremony at the Cathedral Basilica of SS. Peter and Paul on Sept. 7, 2003. PHILADELPHIA DAILY NEWS / G. W. MILLER III

MICHAEL BRYANT                    SARAH J. GLOVER

**Judith Rodin** (left) led the University of Pennsylvania during a 10-year period beginning in 1994, encouraging the school to look outside its borders and help revive its West Philadelphia neighborhood. She was succeeded by Princeton University Provost Amy Gutmann, who became Penn's eighth president in 2004. THE PHILADELPHIA INQUIRER

**For 30 years, Mary Scullion,** a Roman Catholic nun, led an effort to help the city's homeless. The quiet and modest Scullion, a sister in the Mercy order, received the city's prestigious Philadelphia Award in 1991 for her work.

THE PHILADELPHIA INQUIRER / BONNIE WELLER

**Paul Vallas,** who arrived from Chicago to become chief executive officer of the Philadelphia School District in 2003, created a whirlwind of reform in the city's public schools. He departed in 2007 to take over the New Orleans public schools. THE PHILADELPHIA INQUIRER / MICHAEL BRYANT

**Stephen Starr** helped to energize the Philadelphia restaurant scene with a spate of high-concept restaurants that included Buddakan and Morimoto.

THE PHILADELPHIA INQUIRER / ERIC MENCHER

**David Cohen** was a feisty champion of liberal Democratic causes for 37 years on City Council until his death at age 90 in 2005.

THE PHILADELPHIA INQUIRER / TOM GRALISH

**Brian Tierney** led a group of area investors who returned The Inquirer and the Daily News to local ownership in 2006 by purchasing the papers from the McClatchy chain. THE PHILADELPHIA INQUIRER / JOHN COSTELLO

**The father-and-son team** of Ralph and Brian Roberts took Comcast Corp. from a small regional cable provider to a national giant in communications. THE PHILADELPHIA INQUIRER / TOM GRALISH

**State Sen. Vincent Fumo (left),** the powerful South Philadelphia politician, was indicted in 2007 on federal charges, most related to allegedly spending public money for private purposes. Here, he emerges from the federal courthouse with his attorney, Richard Sprague (right).

PHILADELPHIA DAILY NEWS / DAVID MAIALETTI

**Political scandal** is as much a part of Philadelphia as the cheesesteak. In 2003, it was served up again when a listening device, planted by the FBI in Mayor Street's City Hall office, was discovered, revealing an ongoing federal investigation into the mayor and his associates. Focus of the probe fell on Ron White (right), an up-from-the-streets lawyer who became a confidant of and fund-raiser for John Street. White was indicted on influence-peddling charges, but died of cancer in 2004 before he could stand trial. THE PHILADELPHIA INQUIRER / GERALD S. WILLIAMS

**FBI agents carry out boxes** of records from Ron White's Center City office in October 2003. The Bug Scandal, as it came to be called, resulted in a number of indictments and convictions, including that of City Treasurer Corey Kemp. Mayor Street was never charged. PHILADELPHIA DAILY NEWS / YONG KIM

**The city lured the Republican Party** to Philadelphia in 2000 to hold its first national convention in the city since 1948. The GOP nominated George W. Bush, seen here with his wife, Laura, acknowledging the applause of delegates. Bush went on to win election in November, but lost decidedly Democratic Philadelphia to Vice President Al Gore. THE PHILADELPHIA INQUIRER / MICHAEL WIRTZ

**The NAACP came to town** in 2004 to hold its national convention and was addressed by Julian Bond. At the turn of the 20th century, the city was home to W.E.B. DuBois, one of the NAACP's founders, while he researched his classic study, *The Philadelphia Negro*.

PHILADELPHIA DAILY NEWS / JESSICA GRIFFIN

**Philadelphia attracts royalty** of all stripes. The queen of talk television, Oprah Winfrey (center), visited the city in 2003 to accept the Marian Anderson Award for her work on behalf of charity. PHILADELPHIA DAILY NEWS / YONG KIM

**The ripples from the Sept. 11, 2001,** terrorist attacks hit Philadelphia hard. Many of the victims and their relatives lived in the region. One of them was Michael R. Horrocks, a Delaware County native and United Airlines pilot killed when his plane was rammed into the World Trade Center. At a memorial Mass held in Horrocks' hometown of Media, his wife, Miriam (right), and son, Michael, were comforted by the pilot's sister, Jennifer.

THE PHILADELPHIA INQUIRER / ROBERT O. WILLIAMS

**N.J. resident John LaPaglia,** like most other Americans, watched the events unfold on TV.

PHILADELPHIA DAILY NEWS / ALEJANDRO A. ALVAREZ

**Another United pilot** killed in the Sept. 11 attacks was Victor Saracini, a Bucks County native. At his memorial service, a Navy Honor Guard member presented a U.S. flag to his widow, Ellen, and their daughters.

PHILADELPHIA DAILY NEWS / ALEJANDRO A. ALVAREZ

**John Sigmund** (right) holds a picture of his sister, Johanna, who died at the World Trade Center, as he runs down Kelly Drive during the Philadelphia Marathon.

PHILADELPHIA DAILY NEWS / G.W. MILLER III

In the aftermath of 9/11, America invaded Iraq in 2003, hoping for a quick victory and a speedy withdrawal. Instead, the war dragged on for years. (Left) Members of the 424th Army Quartermaster Company, based in Fort Dix, N.J., return after a year of duty in Iraq in 2005. (Right) A Marine from the 772nd Heavy Helicopter Squadron returns to the embrace of his children in 2003. (Below) The remains of Marine Lt. Travis Manion, a Bucks County native, are returned from Iraq to Willow Grove in 2007. THE PHILADELPHIA INQUIRER / DAVID SWANSON

THE PHILADELPHIA INQUIRER / MICHAEL S. WIRTZ

THE PHILADELPHIA INQUIRER / REBECCA BARGER

**Violence can visit** even the most peaceful of places. In October 2006, a local milk truck driver, Charles Carl Roberts IV, invaded an Amish school in Lancaster County and shot 10 girls before turning his gun on himself. Five of the girls died. Six months later, a new school was opened at another site. State troopers protected residents as the investigation continued. THE PHILADELPHIA INQUIRER / ED HILLE

**On a lovely May evening in 2000,** a party was under way in a nightclub on Pier 34 along the Delaware River when part of the pier suddenly gave way, collapsing into the water. Three women, all in their 20s, drowned. In 2007, after one mistrial, the owner and the operator of the pier pleaded guilty to criminal negligence. THE PHILADELPHIA INQUIRER / JOHN COSTELLO

**When diagnosed with cancer** at age 4, Alexandra Scott decided to help the cause of research by setting up a lemonade stand in her front yard. She raised pennies on the first day, but the idea spread. Alex, whose parents moved from Connecticut to Wynnewood to be close to Children's Hospital, died in 2004 at age 8. By then, there were more than 1,000 Alex's Lemonade Stands nationwide.

THE PHILADELPHIA INQUIRER / LINDA JOHNSON

**After living 20 years** as a fugitive in Europe, Ira Einhorn was found in France in 1999 and returned home to stand trial in the death of his girlfriend, Holly Maddux. He was convicted of Maddux's murder after a 2002 trial. THE PHILADELPHIA INQUIRER / CHARLES FOX

**Homicide returned with a vengeance** to Philadelphia at the turn of the new century, as the number of dead climbed until it peaked at more than 400 in one year. Here, members of the Police Department forensic unit examine a shooting scene in North Philadelphia, setting yellow markers near shell casings from 40 bullets fired in a shoot-out. THE PHILADELPHIA INQUIRER / GERALD S. WILLIAMS

**Floods were commonplace,** especially in communities along the Schuylkill and the creeks that fed it. In 2006, Tracy Wright and her boyfriend, Fritz Barnes, had to wade to their house on Walnut Street in the Montgomery County town of Mont Clare. THE PHILADELPHIA INQUIRER / DAVID SWANSON

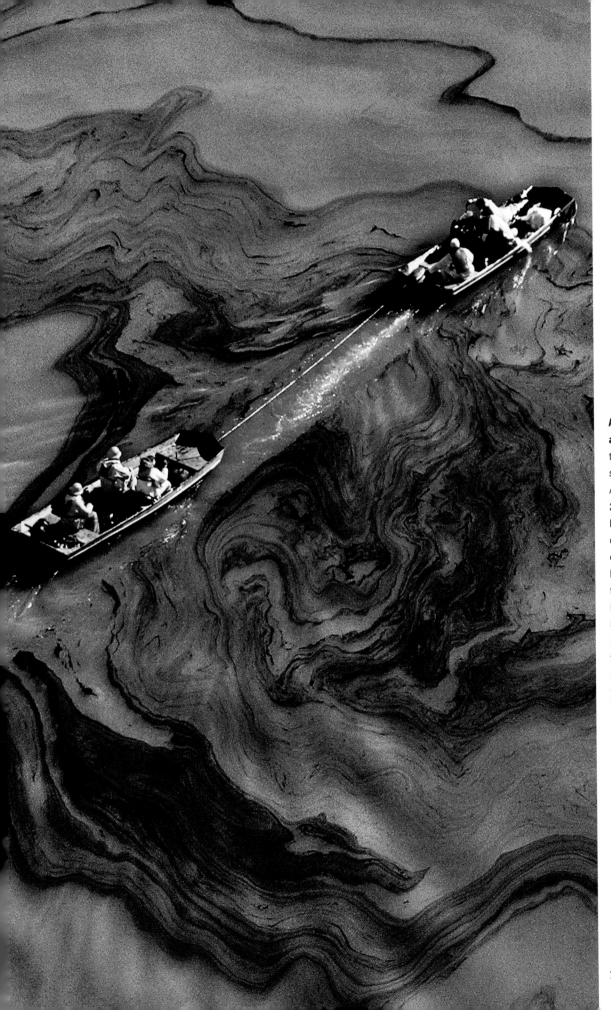

**A shard of an old anchor,** buried in the Delaware River, snagged the tanker Athos I in November 2004, causing it to leak 265,000 gallons of crude oil. It created a 57-mile-long oil slick, from the Tacony-Palmyra Bridge south to Smyrna, Del. Here, crews work the river to clean up the mess.

THE PHILADELPHIA INQUIRER / DAVID SWANSON

**Hundreds of thousands gathered** for the July 2005 Live 8 concert to raise awareness of poverty in Africa. The performances from the steps of the Art Museum were telecast worldwide as part of an eight-city global concert.

THE PHILADELPHIA INQUIRER / PETER TOBIA

**The new century** saw a new generation of Philadelphia entertainers make their mark on the national music scene. Among them were:

**Pink** THE PHILADELPHIA INQUIRER / PETER TOBIA

**Eve** THE PHILADELPHIA INQUIRER / MICHAEL S. WIRTZ

**The Roots** INQUIRER ARCHIVES / ASSOCIATED PRESS

**Jill Scott** THE PHILADELPHIA INQUIRER / PETER TOBIA

**Home to the Phillies and the Eagles since 1971,** Veterans Stadium was no more. The concrete bowl took several years to build but only moments to implode — thanks to the artful placement of explosives by a demolition crew. Thousands gathered to witness the Vet's demise in March 2004. THE PHILADELPHIA INQUIRER / MICHAEL PEREZ

**Lincoln Financial Field** became the Eagles' new home. THE PHILADELPHIA INQUIRER / ERIC MENCHER

**Citizens Bank Park** became home to the Phillies. Both stadiums were built in South Philadelphia, near the site of the Vet. THE PHILADELPHIA INQUIRER / JONATHAN WILSON

**In one painful moment,** during the running of the Preakness in May 2006, the brilliant racing career of Barbaro came to an end. Doctors worked for months to save his life, but the Chester County horse died in January 2007. THE PHILADELPHIA INQUIRER / MICHAEL BRYANT

**Wide receiver Terrell Owens** joined the Eagles in 2004, but his behavior resulted in a suspension, then his release. He was signed by Dallas. THE PHILADELPHIA INQUIRER / JERRY LODRIGUSS

**Allen Iverson** thrilled Sixers fans for 10 seasons before being traded to the Denver Nuggets in 2006. THE PHILADELPHIA INQUIRER / JERRY LODRIGUSS

**Larry Brown** led Iverson and the Sixers to the NBA Finals in 2001. He left in 2003 to become head coach of the Detroit Pistons.

THE PHILADELPHIA INQUIRER / JERRY LODRIGUSS

**Coach John Chaney** took his Temple Owls to the NCAA tournament 17 times before he retired in 2006. PHILADELPHIA DAILY NEWS / STEPHEN M. FALK

**Howard (facing page)** emerged as a
...ies star in his first full season with the team.
...big first baseman was Rookie of the Year
...005 and hit 58 home runs in 2006, earning
...e MVP honors. PHILADELPHIA DAILY NEWS / YONG KIM

**After a dismal decade in the 1990s,** the Eagles got
a new owner in Jeffrey Lurie and a new head coach
in Andy Reid (right), who led the franchise to glory
at the turn of the century. Thanks in large part
to their All-Pro quarterback, Donovan McNabb
(below), the team made it to Super Bowl XXXIX
in 2005, but lost to the New England Patriots, 24-21.

THE PHILADELPHIA INQUIRER / ERIC MENCHER

THE PHILADELPHIA INQUIRER / RON CORTES

# Index

**Fireworks over
the Delaware River**
celebrated the dawn
of a new millennium
on Jan. 1, 2001.